PROPERTY
BURKE CAMPUS LIBRARY
AUGUSTA TECHNICAL COLLEGE

W9-BAH-262

PETERSON'S
PARENT'S
GUIDE TO
THE SAT &
ACT

Peterson's
Parent's
Guide to
the SAT &
ACT

Linda Bizer, Ed.D.
Geraldine Markel, Ph.D.

THOMSON

PETERSON'S™ Australia • Canada • Mexico • Singapore • Spain • United Kingdom • United States

About Thomson Peterson's

Thomson Peterson's (www.petersons.com) is a leading provider of education information and advice, with books and online resources focusing on education search, test preparation, and financial aid. Its Web site offers searchable databases and interactive tools for contacting educational institutions, online practice tests and instruction, and planning tools for securing financial aid. Thomson Peterson's serves 110 million education consumers annually.

For more information, contact Thomson Peterson's, 2000 Lenox Drive, Lawrenceville, NJ 08648; 800-338-3282; or find us on the World Wide Web at: www.petersons.com/about

COPYRIGHT © 2005 Peterson's, a division of Thomson Learning, Inc.
Thomson Learning™ is a trademark used herein under license.

Editor: Fern A. Oram; Production Editor: Megan Hellerman; Copy Editor: Bret Bollman; Proofreader: Teresina Jonkoski; Contributing Editors: Del Franz, Cynthia Johnson, and Drew Johnson; Composition Manager and Interior Design: Michele Able; Manufacturing Manager: Ray Golaszewski; Cover Design: Laura Laus.

ALL RIGHTS RESERVED. No part of this work covered by the copyright herein may be reproduced or used in any form or by any means—graphic, electronic, or mechanical, including photocopying, recording, taping, Web distribution, or information storage and retrieval systems—without the prior written permission of the publisher.

For permission to use material from this text or product, submit a request online at www.thomsonrights.com

Any additional questions about permissions can be submitted by e-mail to thomsonrights@thomson.com

ISBN 0-7689-1823-5

Printed in Canada

10 9 8 7 6 5 4 3 2 1   06 05 04

First Edition

CONTENTS

INTRODUCTION

As a parent, you are concerned about your child's educational future. You have a vested interest in assuring that your teen gets into the college of her choice. Good SAT or ACT scores are an essential part of this process.

Generally, school counselors are charged with the responsibility of assisting and guiding students through the college-admissions process. As counselors, we have spent many years speaking to parent groups and counseling high school students about how to prepare for the SAT and ACT. Over the years, we have also come to realize just how little most parents know about the SAT and ACT. The fact is: The more you know about the tests, the better your teen's chances of succeeding on them will be.

You may believe that SAT and ACT scores are important only at highly selective private colleges, but that is no longer true. Present economic conditions have created situations in which students with very high grades and high college-admissions test scores, who could be admitted to any college, are now applying to state-supported schools in order to keep down the costs of their college education. The result is that state-supported schools are also becoming increasingly selective.

If your teen is applying to a state school that is out-of-state, the stakes are particularly high. He will need to demonstrate both good grades and good test scores in order to be competitive. If your teen's grades are so-so, but his test scores are high, the chances of getting into a good college do still increase.

Here are some myths and truths about the SAT and ACT:

FICTIONS AND FACTS ABOUT COLLEGE-ADMISSIONS TESTS	
FICTION	**FACT**
The SAT and ACT are not important for college admission.	SAT and ACT scores are considered very important factors in college admissions
College-admissions tests don't really count.	Colleges and states offer scholarships based on high SAT and ACT scores.
You can't improve SAT or ACT scores by studying.	Studying can improve scores by hundreds of points.
Studying for and retaking the SAT or ACT is a waste of time and money.	Preparing for the tests and retaking them can increase SAT or ACT scores dramatically.

PREPARATION CAN MAKE A DIFFERENCE

The decision-making process concerning college-admissions tests is often left in the hands of teenagers. What usually happens? College-bound students often take admissions tests and then worry about their test scores, about their grades, and about getting into college. They try to hide their fears and anxieties and appear not to care. When they are uncertain that studying will make a difference, students sometimes feel unmotivated to put forth the effort needed to be successful on these tests.

Since your teen may not automatically communicate information about the SAT or ACT to you, you need to know how to help him in the test-prep process. Your involvement, as a parent with life and work experience, can make a crucial difference in your teen's successful preparation for the tests.

Preparing for the SAT or the ACT does make a difference. Many skills, such as reading, writing, and test-taking speed, can be improved with coaching, practice, and instruction.

WHAT'S IN THIS BOOK

The major purpose of this book is to help you, as a parent, make important decisions regarding the SAT and ACT by giving you accurate information about the tests and about how to create a test-prep plan tailored to the needs you and your teenager have.

This book will guide you through the process step-by-step. Since knowing what's on the tests is crucial, we will describe the SAT and ACT in detail in the first chapter. After familiarizing yourself with the test, your next job will be to choose a role for yourself in helping your teen while she prepares (Chapter 2). In Chapter 3, you'll learn how to pinpoint your teen's strengths and problem areas. After taking a "Pit Stop" for a few words on practice tests, you'll be ready to move on to Chapters 4 through 9, where we'll outline different kinds of test-taking problems and their solutions, including:

- Developing effective work habits
- Using coaches, tutors, and test-prep courses
- Adjusting attitudes
- Improving behaviors
- Addressing challenges for teenagers with disabilities

In Chapters 10 and 11, you'll use all the information you've gathered to create and manage a test-prep plan for you and your teen, whether you have three weeks or three years to prepare. At the end of the book, we'll tell you what your teen needs to do after taking the tests.

Throughout the book, we've provided exercises, charts, and questionnaires for you to use in facilitating the process of creating an effective test-prep plan. We've also included, at the end of the book, additional resources you'll want to consult.

Preparing for the SAT or ACT can be a daunting process. This book will show you how to make your time, patience, and hard work pay off by helping your teenager do the best she can on her college-admissions tests.

Linda Bizer, Ed.D.
Geraldine Markel, Ph.D.

Petersons.com/publishing

Check out our Web site at www.petersons.com/publishing to see if there is any new information regarding any revisions or corrections to the content of this book. We've made sure the information in this book is accurate and up-to-date; however, the test format or content may have changed since the time of publication.

CHAPTER 1

About the SAT and ACT

It's a sure sign that college-admissions testing is a hot issue for teenagers and parents alike when a Hollywood movie focuses on the SAT. *The Perfect Score* depicts a group of teenagers who are so desperate to get into college that they attempt to steal the test in order to ace it. The film points out how competitive the college-admissions process is and the ends to which some students will go to get into the college of their choice.

Obviously, most teenagers would never attempt to steal a test to better their chances of getting into college. However, most teens do need guidance and advice to understand all the testing choices they face and to determine what strategy will best work for them. The process of preparing for standardized tests can be daunting. So, let's get started in guiding your teen through the challenges of college-admissions testing.

WHAT ARE THE SAT AND ACT (AND ALL THOSE OTHER TESTS)?

Almost all high school students applying to U.S. colleges need to take either the SAT or ACT. Most colleges (except for a handful that don't require a college-admissions test) use scores from the SAT and ACT to make decisions about which students to admit. The scores are also used to determine monetary scholarships. Obviously, a lot rides on these scores, and both you and your teenager need to understand the tests and the options available for preparing for these tests.

Actually, your teen will probably take numerous tests as part of the college-admissions process. There are not only the SAT and the ACT, but also the PSAT and the PLAN—tests that students usually take before tackling the SAT and ACT. In this book we'll focus on the most crucial of these tests: the SAT and the ACT.

However, we will not only give the information you need to know about the SAT and ACT, but we'll also explain the role of the PSAT, PLAN, and other tests in the college-admissions process.

What's on the SAT?

First administered in 1926, the SAT (pronounced S-A-T, not "sat") originally focused on measuring innate reasoning ability. It used to be called the Scholastic Aptitude Test, but today the letters no longer stand for anything. It's officially now designated the SAT Reasoning Test, but is generally just called "the SAT."

Who Creates the SAT?

The SAT is owned and administered by the College Board, based in New York City. However, the test is developed by the Educational Testing Service (ETS) in Princeton, New Jersey. More information about the SAT is available from the College Board:

College Board
45 Columbus Avenue
New York, NY 10023-6992
212-713-8000
www.collegeboard.com

Over the years, the SAT has changed significantly. The most recent revision of the SAT resulted in the addition of a Writing section—including an essay—and changes to both the content that is covered and the types of questions used in the Math and Critical Reading (previously "Verbal") sections of the test. Students taking the SAT in spring 2005 or later will take this new SAT exam that, according to the College Board, "assesses student reasoning based on knowledge and skills developed by the student in school coursework."

So, the SAT now has three sections: Critical Reading, Mathematics, and Writing. The Critical Reading section (70 minutes, divided into 3 parts) consists of reading passages, both short (50–100 words) and long (600–900 words) in length. There is at least one fiction passage on every test. Some test questions include literary concepts and terminology, such as simile and personification. The Critical Reading section also has some sentence completion questions, where students must correctly determine the answer choice that best completes a sentence. Tests administered after January 2005 no longer have the Analogies section, in which students had to choose a pair of words related to each other in the same way as a given pair of words; this change greatly reduces the importance of vocabulary in determining SAT scores.

The Mathematics section (70 minutes, divided into 3 parts) consists of multiple-choice questions as well as some open-ended questions. Some questions pertain to Algebra II, which is the third year of most high school mathematics sequences. Thus, in addition to the basic math concepts (fractions, decimals, area of a circle, etc.) that are covered, the Mathematics section may have questions relating to such advanced topics as linear functions, manipulations with exponents, and properties of tangent lines. The quantitative comparisons, the often-tricky questions that focus on determining whether the quantity in Column A was larger or smaller than the quantity represented in Column B, were also eliminated in the most recent redesign of the SAT.

The Writing section (60 minutes, divided into 3 parts) of the test is designed to assess basic writing skills. This entire section was added to the SAT in 2005. Two parts of the writing section include multiple-choice items testing the student's knowledge of grammar. The third part is a 25-minute essay on an assigned topic. This essay question, referred to as the "essay prompt," is open-ended and requires that a student take a position on an issue and support it with examples from school or general experience. No prior knowledge is required in order to respond to the essay prompt.

The SAT also includes a 25-minute experimental section in which new questions are tested for validity. The order of the different parts of the SAT varies, and this section can appear anywhere in the test, so there's no way students taking the test can really determine which section of the test is the experimental one. Thus, the best advice is to do one's best on all parts of the test.

So, including the experimental section, the SAT clocks in at 3 hours, 45 minutes in length.

A Penalty for Guessing

The phrase "guessing penalty" has to do with the way many standard-ized tests are scored. For instance, consider a multiple-choice test with five answer choices for every question: (A), (B), (C), (D), and (E). Coco the Chimp takes the test and answers "(C)" for every problem, since Coco likes that letter. On a 100-question test, Coco usually will get 20 questions correct just by guessing randomly, since, statistically speaking one-fifth of the answers will be (C).

It doesn't look good to have a chimpanzee scoring that well, so many tests have a guessing penalty that deducts points for any wrong answer. Let's say Coco gets 1 point for every correct answer. But there is a guess-ing penalty of $\frac{1}{4}$ point for every wrong answer, so Coco's score would then be:

20 correct answers × 1 point = 20 points

0.25 penalty × 80 incorrect answers = 20

20 points for correct answers − 20 points for incorrect guesses = 0 points total

So, the guessing penalty eliminates Coco's reward for guessing randomly.

The SAT has just such a guessing penalty. Thus, on the SAT, students should never guess randomly. However, if they can eliminate one of the answer choices as incorrect and are guessing only among the remaining choices, the odds improve and they should go ahead and guess. The more answer choices that can eliminated, the better their guessing will be.

What's on the ACT?

The ACT was first administered in 1959. The letters formerly referred to the American College Testing Program, but the test is now officially simply called the ACT Assessment (pronounced A-C-T, not "act"). The test focuses on achievement, rather than aptitude; questions are drawn from content material covered in the secondary school curriculum. The test consists entirely of multiple-choice questions. There is no guessing penalty, so students should never leave an answer blank, even if they are guessing totally at random.

Who Creates the ACT?

The ACT Assessment is developed and administered by ACT, a nonprofit organization based in Iowa City, Iowa. Registration materials and information about the test are available from the ACT:

ACT
500 ACT Drive
P.O. Box 168
Iowa City, IA 52243-0168
319-337-1000
www.act.org

The ACT includes 215 multiple-choice questions. Expect it to last about 4 hours, including breaks, instructions, and the interest inventory—an exercise used for career and educational planning. The actual test time is 2 hours, 55 minutes and includes:

- **English**   75 questions   45 minutes
- **Math**   60 questions   60 minutes
- **Reading**   40 questions   35 minutes
- **Science**   40 questions   35 minutes

In 2005, the ACT began to offer an optional written essay designed to be administered when the regular ACT is taken; it added 30 minutes to the test time. The ACT decided to provide students with this essay option since a number of colleges had begun requiring a student essay administered in a standardized testing environment. This allows colleges requiring the SAT with its new essay component to continue to accept ACT scores as well. Teens need to check with the colleges to which they are applying to see if the writing test is required.

The SAT and ACT as an Early Indicator of Academic Talent

Junior high or middle school students identified by their schools as academically talented may be invited to participate in a talent search program that includes taking the SAT or ACT. Some of the programs include:

- Midwest Talent Search at Northwestern University
- Rocky Mountain Talent Search at University of Denver
- Talent Identification Program at Duke University
- Center for Talented Youth at Johns Hopkins University

Parents should contact the guidance counselor at their teen's school for more information about these programs and the special SAT and ACT registration procedures.

What Are the SAT Subject Tests?

The SAT Subject Tests (formerly called the SAT II Subject Tests) are a series of 1-hour tests administered five times a year, usually on the same test-administration dates as the SAT. The College Board adds new SAT Subject Tests from time to time and occasionally removes a subject from those offered. Recently discontinued was the SAT II Writing test (last administration January, 2005) since the content in that test is now included in the Writing section of the SAT. As of press time, the following SAT Subject Tests are offered by the College Board (check the College Board Web site, www.collegeboard.com, for the most up-to-date offerings):

- **English:** Literature
- **History:** World History and U.S. History
- **Languages:** Chinese, French, German, Modern Hebrew, Italian, Japanese, Korean, Latin, and Spanish.
- **Math:** Level I and II
- **Science:** Biology E (Ecological), Biology M (Molecular), Chemistry, and Physics

Each college and university sets its own SAT Subject Test requirements, so you'll need to check with the colleges to which your teen is considering applying. Sometimes a college will require that incoming students take a specific SAT Subject Test, but often a college will only ask for results from 1–3 tests and the student can pick which subject test(s) to take. Other colleges make the Subject Tests optional and include those scores in the student's application. If your teen is exceptional in a particular subject area, it can't hurt to submit SAT Subject Test scores, even if they are not required.

Remember, while the SAT rates overall reasoning abilities and skills in math, reading, and writing, the SAT Subject Tests measure student knowledge in specific subject areas. The subject tests provide colleges with another tool to measure student qualifications, and some colleges do require students to take one or more of these subject tests, along with the SAT or ACT.

AP and CLEP

AP (Advanced Placement) tests, like the SAT Subject Tests, test the student's knowledge of specific subject areas. Reaching a certain score on an AP test entitles the student to college credit at most colleges and universities; check the AP policy of the colleges your teenager is considering. While taking AP courses in high school—and getting good grades in these courses—will help a student's admission prospects, usually the score received on an AP test itself is not used in the college-admissions process. SAT Subject Tests, in contrast, were created to provide colleges and universities with more information on applicants in the college-admissions process, but doing well on an SAT Subject Test does not translate into college credit. Thus, high school students often take both the SAT Subject Test and the AP test for the same subject area.

At most colleges, CLEP (College-Level Examination Program) subject tests are a way to get credit for the knowledge and experience a student already has, even if he never took an AP course in high school. Even if credit is not granted, doing well on a CLEP test may allow the student to skip an introductory-level college course.

More information on the AP tests and the CLEP is available online at www.collegeboard.com.

What Is the PSAT/NMSQT?

The PSAT/NMSQT (Preliminary SAT/National Merit Scholarship Qualifying Test) is an assessment of reading, writing, and mathematic ability designed to give students some idea of what it's like to take the SAT. Students usually take the PSAT in their junior year of high school; the test is administered only once a year—in October. Scores are not sent to colleges. After taking the PSAT, students automatically receive a copy of their test booklet, their results, and the publisher's correct answers.

This 2-hour test is similar to the SAT and uses questions from previous SATs. However, there is no essay on the PSAT and, since high school juniors are typically just beginning Algebra II in October of their junior year, the PSAT does not include most of the Algebra II topics found on the SAT. Just like the SAT, the PSAT has a penalty for guessing incorrectly.

Students, parents, and school personnel frequently attach little importance to the PSAT because they consider it only a practice test. This belief is partly correct, as the scores don't count toward college admission. However, PSAT scores are important for other reasons. In addition to preparing students for the SAT, the test also functions as the National Merit Scholarship Qualifying Test (NMSQT). Students that do well on the PSAT are entered into the competition to become National Merit Scholars. Besides being used to determine eligibility for National Merit Scholarships, PSAT scores may also be used for state-supported financial awards and a variety of special scholarships. So while a good PSAT score won't help your teen get into college, it might help *pay* for college. Depending on your point of view, this might make the PSAT just as important as the SAT.

An increasing number of students are taking the PSAT earlier than the fall of their junior year and using the results to assess how they will do on the SAT. The earlier students take and analyze the results of the PSAT, the more time they have to prepare for the SAT.

The PLAN

The PLAN is a 10th-grade pre-ACT assessment program designed to help students improve their planning and preparation for postsecondary education. Similar to the ACT, the PLAN contains tests of English, math, reading, and science reasoning. The PLAN does not include the essay option now offered with the ACT. Similar to the PSAT, PLAN scores are not sent to colleges.

But the PLAN is more than just a preliminary ACT. One useful feature of this examination is the career inventory, since it may be the first time teens receive information of this sort in a printed, systematic format. And, like the PSAT, scores on the PLAN can be used to qualify for a number of scholarships.

SAT OR ACT: WHICH TEST TO TAKE?

One key question facing college-bound teens is whether to take the SAT or ACT. Approximately 1.4 million students in the high school graduating class of 2004 took the SAT and almost 1.2 million students took the ACT. For the most part, which of these two tests students signed up for depends on the region of the United States in which they lived. The SAT dominates in the Northeast and on the West Coast, while the ACT is the test students in the Midwest and South generally take.

Since colleges in the United States usually try to attract a geographically diverse student body, virtually all of them accept either SAT or ACT scores. Only a handful of colleges insist on one test and not the other, and this list of colleges is dwindling. Even colleges that claim to prefer one test over the other seldom discriminate against applicants who take the "other" test. Teens should check the requirements of the schools in which they are interested in applying to; they probably will find that they have the choice of taking either the SAT or ACT.

The Options

In order to determine which test will work best for them, teens need to understand both the SAT and ACT and how the two tests differ. Keep in mind, too, that there is not only the option of taking either the SAT or ACT, but also the option of taking both of them. While this option may require more test-taking stamina and more money in test-registration fees, it offers a way to make certain that your teen takes the test that will present his capabilities in the best possible light. Taking both tests allows students the option of deciding which test scores—SAT or ACT—they will submit with their college application.

The SAT and ACT Compared

With the most recent revision of the SAT, the differences between the two tests have decreased. But there are still some important differences you should be aware of in guiding you teen in choosing which test to take.

The Guessing Penalty

There is no penalty for guessing on the ACT exam, while there is one on the SAT. On the ACT, students can guess on the multiple-choice questions they don't know or have time for; the likelihood is that at least a few of their guesses will be correct. On the SAT, such a strategy will not work, and it may even reduce scores, since points are subtracted from the raw score for incorrect answers, but not for questions left blank.

It might seem that this makes the ACT easier or better than the SAT. However, this is not true. Both the SAT and ACT are "normed," meaning your teen's final score on either test is derived by comparing his performance with that of other students taking the exam. On the ACT, since there's no guessing penalty for *anyone*, there's no advantage gained. To visualize this, imagine a thousand people lined up side-by-side in one long parallel line. If everyone moves forward two feet (no guessing penalty!), no one gains any ground on anyone else.

Math and Science

If math is not a strong point for your teenager, you should remember that the math section accounts for a third of the SAT score, but only a fourth of the ACT score. On the other hand, if your teen does well in advanced math courses, like Algebra II, it may be advantageous for him to take the SAT, since only the SAT has questions covering advanced Algebra.

The SAT has no science section, but the ACT does. So if your teenager does well in science, it may be advantageous for her to take the ACT.

The Essay

The essay is a required part of the SAT, but an optional component of the ACT. Of course, since many colleges require the essay, students may not be able to avoid it. But check with the colleges to which your teen is applying; if they don't require the essay and you don't think your teen would do well on the essay, he can probably skip it. But, if writing is your teenager's thing and he is better at it than most students, you should encourage him to take either the SAT or the ACT with the optional writing test.

Score Reporting

The student who takes the ACT test more than once can specify which test scores (probably the highest ones!) she wants reported to colleges. If a student takes the SAT more than once, all her test scores will be reported to all the colleges to which she applies. In other words, with the ACT, scores from a particular test date can be deleted permanently from your teen's record; this can't be done with the SAT.

General Factors

The questions on the ACT are directly related to what students have learned in their high school English, math, and science courses. For this reason, some students are more comfortable with the ACT than the SAT. However, if your teen has strong analytic, organizational, verbal, and writing skills, he will probably do better on the SAT. Also, remember that the SAT is about an hour longer than the ACT. If your teen has strong attention and concentration skills, you may want to encourage taking the SAT. Likewise, if concentration for such a long period will be a problem, you may want to encourage him to take the ACT.

COMPARING THE SAT TO THE ACT		
	SAT	**ACT**
PURPOSE	To assess student reasoning based on the knowledge and skills developed by the student in school coursework	To measure student achievement based on school curriculum
REGIONAL DOMINANCE	Northeastern and western states	Midwestern and southern states
WHEN OFFERED	Offered 5 times a year	Offered 5 times a year
PARTS OF THE TEST	3 Parts: Writing, Critical Reading, and Mathematics	4 Parts: English, Mathematics, Reading, and Science
LENGTH	3 hours, 45 minutes	2 hours, 55 minutes
ESSAY REQUIREMENT	60-minute Writing section, including a 25-minute student essay	Essay not required; optional 30-minute essay is offered
MATH LEVEL	Mathematics section includes Algebra II content	Mathematics section does not include Algebra II content.
MULTIPLE SCORE REPORTING	Can be taken multiple times; the last 6 scores are reported to colleges	Can be taken multiple times; only the scores from the selected test date are reported to colleges
GUESSING	Small penalty to discourage random guessing	No penalty for guessing

HOW MANY TIMES SHOULD THE SAT OR ACT BE TAKEN?

Teens can take the SAT or ACT as many times as they want. Many take the tests twice, first as a junior and again as a senior. Twice is usually enough, unless the student is going to take more time to prepare for the test, get new or specialized tutoring, or was ill or under stress during the times he previously took the test. According to the College Board, 55 percent of the juniors taking the test got better scores when they took the test again as seniors, 35 percent did worse the second time, and 10 percent stayed the same. So, in general, there is little to lose (except the registration fee) and much to be gained by taking the test more than once. Increasingly, that is becoming the norm.

You should encourage your teenager to take the test in the spring of his junior year. This allows time for some type of test prep and retaking the test, if the scores are not what you and your teen were hoping for.

Taking the SAT More Than Once

The College Board sends all of a student's SAT scores to the colleges to which he is applying, but most colleges use only the highest score the student obtained in their admissions formulas. However, there are some colleges that average the scores in their admissions formulas, or use only the most recent SAT score. Check with each college to obtain their policies regarding multiple SAT test scores.

Students who had problems during the test, such as misunderstanding the directions, feeling physically ill, or putting their answers on the wrong place on the answer sheet may want to consider canceling their scores. If a student cancels her score, it is as if the student had never taken the test, and neither the student nor the college ever finds out how the student did. If your teenager cancels her scores, all scores—Writing, Critical Reading, and Mathematics—on that test date are canceled. Scores can be canceled at the test center before leaving the room or by submitting a request in writing by the Wednesday immediately after the test date.

Taking the ACT More Than Once

The incentive to take the test more than once is even greater for the ACT. The reason: If a student has taken the test more than once, ACT policies allow the student to select which test date's scores will be submitted to the college-admissions offices. Thus, colleges only get to see a student's best scores. However, keep in mind that the scores submitted to the college have to be from the same test date for all four parts of the test; students can't submit a math score from one date and a science score from another. Students may have a particular test date's scores entirely deleted by sending the request in writing to: ACT Records, P.O. Box 451, Iowa City, IA 52243-0451.

ACT research shows that of the students who took the ACT more than once 55 percent improved their composite score on the retest, 22 percent had no change in their composite score when they took the test again, and 23 percent experienced a decrease in their composite score on the retest.

UNDERSTANDING SCORES

Although SAT and ACT scores seem totally different at first glance, the scores on both tests are derived through the same process, called "norming." Students' SAT or ACT scores are determined by computing how one student did compared to other students who took the test. Thus, a student's "raw score," based on the number of right and wrong answers, is translated into a test score that tells where the student falls in the statistical curve reflecting all test-takers. The test administrator doesn't reveal the raw score, so students don't know how many answers they got right or wrong, just how they did compared to other test-takers.

Probably the best way to understand your teen's SAT or ACT score is to look at the percentile, or rank, to which the score corresponds. The percentile is included in the score report from the testing organization. A score in the 95th percentile means the student ranked above 95 percent of the students taking the test. A score in the 50th percentile means the student scored higher than 50 percent of the students taking the test.

What the SAT Scores Mean

SAT scores range from 200 to a high score of 800 on each section. The total SAT score is obtained by adding the scores on all three sections, so a perfect score—there's that movie again!—is 2400. The lowest score possible, even if every answer is wrong, is 600.

As mentioned earlier, a guessing penalty, designed to penalize random guessing, is factored into the raw scores on the different sections of the SAT. There is a penalty of $\frac{1}{4}$ point for each multiple-choice question answered incorrectly, but no penalty for questions left blank. If students can eliminate one of more of the answer choices as obviously wrong answers, they should still guess. If the test-taker has no idea which answer is correct or hasn't had time to read the question, it is best to leave the question blank.

For the high school graduating class of 2004, the average SAT score on the Mathematics section was 518 and the average score on the Verbal section was 508. This combines for an average score of 1026, out of the 1600 points possible, before the addition of the Writing section of the SAT. The Mathematics and Critical Reading tests offered in 2005, of course, are somewhat different from the previous Mathematics and Verbal tests but, based on preliminary testing of questions in practice administrations of the test, the College Board has scaled the scores on the new tests so that scores will be comparable.

Scoring on the new Writing section of the SAT is more complicated. Two subscores are given for the writing section: One subscore, on a scale of 20–80, indicates how the student did on the multiple-choice questions and an essay subscore, on a scale of 2–12, indicates how the student did on the essay. The essay score of 2–12 is based on the scores given by two essay readers who each assign the essay a score from 1– 6. A score of 1 represents very poor organization and development, while a 6 indicates very good organization, facility with language, and insightfulness. The scores of the two graders are added together to provide the essay subscore. Then the essay subscore and the multiple-choice subscore are combined and scaled to provide a SAT Writing section score, on a 200- to 800-point scale.

Colleges to which the student requests that SAT results be sent will not only get scores, but will also get access to a copy of the student's actual SAT essay. Besides helping to make a decision on college admission, the essay score—and the actual essay—may be used by the college to place a student in the appropriate level of English composition courses.

What the ACT Scores Mean

Students receive a score for each of the four tests (English, Reading, Mathematics, and Science). The scoring ranges from a low of 1 to a high of 36. These scores are averaged to provide a composite ACT score that also ranges from 1–36. Only about one out of every 5,000 students who takes the ACT earns a composite score of 36. The national average composite score was 20.9 for the high school graduating class of 2004, up from a national average of 20.8 for the graduating class of 2003. As expected, most students score near the middle of the scale, with few at either extreme. In fact, using statistics for the high school graduating classes of 2002, 2003, and 2004, a score of 32 or above ranks in the 99th percentile, and a score of 11 or below puts the student in the lowest percentile. A score of 24 puts the student above the 75th percentile, and a score 16 or below places the student with the lowest 25 percent taking the test.

In addition, the student taking the ACT receives seven subscores, ranging from 1–18, that are designed to provide additional feedback regarding his strengths and weaknesses. For example, in the reading test, he will receive a subscore for social studies and science reading skills and a subscore for arts and literature reading skills. These subscores, however, are not very important in the admissions decisions of colleges and universities, which generally use only the four subject test scores and/or the composite score.

At press time, scoring procedures and scales for the new optional ACT Writing Test had not been announced.

A Note on SAT Subject Test Scores

SAT Subject Tests are also reported on a scale from 200–800. These scores tell college-admissions staff members how one student did compared to other students who took the test. Like the score reported on the regular SAT, students will not know how many questions were answered either correctly or incorrectly on the SAT Subject Tests. Average scores on the SAT Subject Tests vary widely, with the highest being 756 on the Chinese with Listening Subject Test and 745 on the Korean with Listening Subject Test. Average scores on the more popular SAT Subject Tests are 603 on the U.S. History Subject Test, 586 on the Mathematics Level I Subject Test, and 584 on the Biology E (Ecological) Subject Test.

What the PSAT Scores Mean

PSAT score reports provide scores on a scale from 20–80 for each section of the test (Critical Reading, Math, and Writing). The average critical reading, math, and writing skills score for juniors is 49. Also on the score report is the Selection Index, which is the sum of the three scores. The Selection Index ranges from 60–240, with an average of 147.

Score reports also include percentiles, allowing students to compare scores with those of other juniors applying to college. For example, a student with a percentile of 53 has earned a score better than 53 out of every 100 college-bound juniors who took the test.

What the PLAN Scores Mean

The PLAN is scored on a scale of 1–32, rather than the 1–36 score range of the ACT itself. Students taking the PLAN receive a score for each of the four subjects tested on the ACT (English, Mathematics, Reading, and Science), plus a composite score that is also on a 1–32 scale. In order to compare a student's performance to that of other college-bound 10th-graders, percentile rankings for all five of these scores are provided. In addition, the score report includes a predicted range of how the student will score on the actual ACT. To help identify strengths and weaknesses, the score report contains subscores for the English and math sections, providing feedback on more specific skill areas.

What Are Good Scores on the SAT and ACT?

It's difficult to say exactly what a "good" score is on either test. What is considered a high score at one institution may be below average at another. However, colleges usually provide score information for their most recent, incoming freshman class. Using this, you can see how your teen's scores compare to those of students admitted by the school the previous year. Since test scores from one year to the next at a college or university remain fairly constant, you can get a reasonable idea of just how "good" your teenager's score will be at a particular school.

Some colleges and universities report the average SAT and ACT scores of their incoming freshman class. Most, however, report ranges, usually the range of the SAT and ACT scores of the middle 50 percent of their incoming students. Although it may seem more complicated, the range information gives you a much better idea of how your teen would fit into the incoming freshman class.

In the end, whether a high school student considers her score on the SAT or ACT "good" depends on a variety of factors. Among these are whether or not the student feels she met her parents' expectations, how she did compared to her friends, and how the score compares to the range expected by the colleges to which she is applying.

What Has Made Scores on the SAT and ACT So Important?

There are two major reasons for the increasing importance the SAT and ACT play in determining admission to college.

For one thing, teacher recommendations, previously considered a valuable part of the college application, have decreased in value. The Family Educational Rights and Privacy Act (1974), which allows students (18 years and older) and parents to examine all documents in the student's personal folder, has affected some teachers' willingness to write frank and honest recommendations.

Grade inflation is the second factor. A grade of "A" today in many schools is like the dollar—not worth what it used to be. The value of grades, as predictors of college performance, is seriously reduced by grade inflation, as well as by grading standards that vary from school to school. Therefore, colleges faced with questions about grades and teacher recommendations are left with one "objective" measure: SAT or ACT scores.

How Colleges Use SAT and ACT Scores

Both you and your teenager should remember that the SAT or ACT score is never the sole criterion for college admissions and, at many schools, not even the most important factor; schools look at a variety of criteria. The SAT and ACT were never designed to tell everything about a student. One key missing ingredient in a test score is motivation.

Consider Paul, a bright but unmotivated student. He cuts class, doesn't complete his homework, and gets poor grades. His score on the ACT is 31. Clearly, this is a high score and could be considered "good." Yet, if this score was used alone, it might not accurately predict Paul's academic performance in college. In the end, in spite of his high test score, Paul was rejected by the most competitive colleges.

Now consider Delia. She is highly motivated, participates in several extracurricular activities, and has an excellent grade point average—in fact, she was school valedictorian. But she earned a 400 on the verbal part of the SAT, which could clearly be considered a "low" score. As with Paul, if Delia's score was used alone, it might not accurately predict her college performance. Delia's low verbal score did not prevent her from being admitted to a college classified as "most competitive."

The following list shows factors generally considered in the admission process by four-year public and private institutions. These factors are not ranked in order of importance:

- High school grades and class rank
- Out-of-class accomplishments
- Personal qualities, such as leadership, motivation, or special abilities
- High school recommendations
- Personal essay or autobiography
- Personal interview
- Academic preparation, as evidenced in subject area achievement test scores and the difficulty of the high school courses that were taken
- SAT or ACT scores

Each college and university uses a different process to evaluate applicants; as a result, the importance of SAT and ACT scores, relative to other factors, varies at each institution. You should not hesitate to ask schools about the role of SAT and ACT scores in their admissions process.

A recent survey of colleges and universities reported that both grades and college-admissions test scores are the two most important factors in college admissions. Regarding these two factors, more than 50 percent of the schools reported that the college-admissions test score is a very important factor, while only about 40 percent of public and private colleges reported that grades are a very important factor. Furthermore, about 40 percent of colleges indicate having minimum SAT or ACT score requirements. While you should recognize that test scores are not the only criterion in college admissions, the importance of SAT and ACT scores at most colleges and universities in the United States should not be underplayed.

SAT and ACT scores are among the most important factors in college admissions partly because they provide an easy, practical way to sort college applications. Imagine all the applications for a particular college stacked into a single pile. This pile, as you might expect, would reach several stories high at some colleges. The admissions personnel want to do the best job they can, but they also want to work less than 120 hours a week. Setting minimum SAT and ACT scores offers a fast, simple way to weed through the pile. After the first cut, the remaining applicants are often sorted into categories by SAT or ACT scores. The high scores are looked over first and these applicants get viewed in a favorable light, since colleges often use test scores as a way to trumpet the academic excellence of their college. After the high-score applicants are reviewed, the medium scorers get reviewed, but by now the number of open slots for admission has dwindled. Finally, the low-score pile gets sifted through and the number of available openings is even smaller. In the end, everyone above the minimum score gets looked at and evaluated, but high-scoring students often get looked at first, simply as a matter of logistics. This gives them a better chance of getting accepted by the college, even when many factors other than SAT and ACT scores are considered in the admissions process.

SPECIAL CONSIDERATIONS AND ACCOMMODATIONS

Both the College Board and the ACT offer special accommodations for students with disabilities. And both organizations offer their tests not only in the United States, but around the world.

Some circumstances warrant special conditions for test administration. These include students with documented disabilities, those with religious beliefs that prohibit Saturday testing, and students who are homebound or confined. Special accommodations include Sunday testing, standard-time testing with accommodation, extended-time testing, and special individualized testing with extended-time and alternate formats available. More information is available at high school guidance offices or the test-makers' Web sites. Chapter 8, in this book, focuses on teenagers with disabilities.

Also note that accommodations can be made for students who cannot afford the test registration fee. Testing fees are waived for qualified students. More information is available at the test administration Web sites previously listed.

The SAT and ACT in Foreign Countries

American students living and studying abroad are allowed to take the SAT and ACT on regular test-administration dates at centers located in countries around the world. Foreign students who are interested in applying to colleges in the United States can also take the SAT and ACT in these same centers.

For the SAT, students use the same online registration process as do students in the United States. The only exceptions are for testing in several African countries.

However, for the ACT, another registration process applies for students who wish to take the test outside the United States. Students must obtain a special registration packet and register directly with the supervisor of the test center where they wish to test, not with ACT and not via the Web. A full listing of test centers, including telephone and fax numbers, is available online at the ACT Web site.

A Spanish version of the SAT is available only in Puerto Rico for students going to Spanish-language colleges and universities. The ACT is offered only in English.

CHAPTER 2
Choosing Your Role

GETTING INVOLVED

The first step in creating a plan to help your teen prepare for college-admissions tests is to define your role. As a parent, you already play a variety of roles in raising your children, wearing different hats at different times. You may find yourself acting as mentor, chauffeur, cook, coach, mediator, or even prison warden. All of these roles require different time commitments and often even require you to acquire new skills.

When it comes to helping your teen tackle the SAT or ACT, you might feel confused about which role to take. Many parents find becoming involved with their teen's education a bit challenging. Teenagers can have a hard time accepting their parents as teachers. Sometimes, when parents try to teach their teen, their efforts lead to the three "Fs": *failure*, *friction*, and *frustration*. When these experiences arise, parents may conclude that they have no role to play in their child's education.

Of course, nothing could be further from the truth. In fact, there are many roles parents should choose to play in helping their teens prepare for college-admissions tests. In this chapter, we show you some of the roles you can assume in your effort to successfully teach your teen.

Educators and legislators recognize the importance of having parents involved in their children's education. Research shows that parents can successfully teach their teens, when they have been taught how to do it.

ROLES FOR PARENTS

You can play a variety of roles in helping your teen prepare for college-admissions tests. In guiding your teen, you may choose to be one, or any combination, of the following:

- Buyer
- Advocate
- Supporter
- Helper
- Organizer
- Manager
- Tutor

Let's look at how each of these roles relates to SAT and ACT preparation.

The Buyer

"Here's a check to buy the ACT books you want."

This parent feels that it is the teenager's job to prepare for college-admissions tests and the parent's job is to offer financial support. The teenager is the main decision-maker and is responsible for obtaining the necessary materials and services. This parental role is supportive and not too time-consuming, although it may present problems for parents who are on a tight budget.

The Advocate

"How does your school help 11th-graders prepare for the SAT or ACT?"

This parent believes that it is the school's job to prepare students for the test. The parent starts the ball rolling and requests information from school personnel about what services are available. The teenager may or may not be involved in this information-gathering process. Most parents feel comfortable in this role, as it requires little time and is accepted by both school personnel and teachers.

The Supporter

"I know it's a tough test. I see you're working hard and spending a lot of time studying for it."

This parent believes that the teenager has the major responsibility in preparing for the test. The teenager is the decision-maker, and the parent offers suggestions and support. The parent is understanding, empathetic, and non-critical. This can be a comfortable parental role since it is non-threatening to the teenager, is positive, and requires a minimal amount of time.

The Helper

"I picked up this SAT practice book and made a list of some tutoring courses for you."

This parent believes that it is the parent's job to help the teenager with his plans, but that it is up to the teenager to make the final decisions. This parent only helps when asked and follows the teen's timetable when possible. This is a comfortable role since it is supportive, non-threatening, and not time-consuming. However, this role might pose problems for working parents who do not have flexible schedules.

The Organizer

"I've signed you up to take a test-prep course."

This parent feels that the teenager should not be responsible for the arrangements involved in test preparation. The parent assumes a major role in establishing a timetable, finding out about resources, arranging for services, and purchasing materials. The teenager's responsibility is to follow the parent's game plan. In short, the parent provides the framework so that the teenager can spend her time preparing effectively. This role is time-consuming and parent-directed.

The Manager

"After you study your vocabulary words for 30 minutes, you can use the car."

This parent believes that good intentions are not enough to make her child perform well on the SAT. She believes in the rule "work first, then play." Firm guidelines and consequences are established to keep the ball rolling. The degree to which the teenager is involved in planning and implementing this approach depends on a number of factors, such as the teenager's maturity and motivation.

Your comfort with this role is related to the extent to which you believe in the "work first, then play" philosophy. If you already ascribe to this rule in raising your children, extending it to SAT or ACT test preparation will be an easy task. Patience and willingness to check on study behavior are also important factors to consider when thinking about the role of manager.

The Tutor

"I'll explain the Algebra problem to you."

Parents who take on the role of tutor believe that they can work effectively with their teenagers on academic subjects. These parents offer direct instruction in one or more of the SAT or ACT areas, such as vocabulary, reading comprehension, geometry, or science.

Remember no single role is superior to the other. Find the roles that are best suited to you and your teenager's needs.

WHICH ROLE IS FOR YOU?

Defining your role requires two steps:

- Collecting information about yourself
- Using this information systematically, as you decide which role you want to take on and when

To collect information about yourself, take the following "Parent Survey."

PARENT SURVEY

Directions: Read each question and circle the answer that best describes you. You may find that you mark some questions low, others medium, and still others high.

	LOW	MEDIUM	HIGH
1. How much money is available for test preparation, tutoring, books, etc.?	Up to $25 for books	$25–$150 for books and tutoring	More than $150 for courses, books, etc.
2. Do you question school personnel?	Never. I feel uncomfortable.	Sometimes, if it is important.	Usually. It's my right.
3. Do you make supportive statements about academic achievements?	Not usually. I don't want to spoil my child.	Sometimes, if grades are good.	Frequently, especially about trying hard.
4. What resources are available in your school or community?	I don't have the faintest idea!	I thought I saw an advertisement for an SAT course.	I know a tutor and saw an SAT book in the store.
5. How involved do you feel?	I don't know if I should be involved.	I'll do what I can if I'm asked.	This is important! I'll help whenever I can.
6. How much time are you willing to devote to SAT preparation?	1–3 hours total	1–2 hours per week	3 or more hours per week
7. How efficient is your decision-making?	It's either too slow or too hasty.	Sometimes good, but it's a tiresome process.	Usually good. I consider options and select one.
8. Who should be the primary decision-maker?	Not me. It's not my job!	I'll make decisions sometimes.	Me. I have more experience.
9. How organized are you?	I lose papers, forget dates, and am often late.	I write schedules but forget to follow them.	A place for everything and everything in its place!
10. How comfortable are you with your teenager?	It's tough being around my child.	Some days are good, others aren't.	Minor problems, but we get along.
11. How firm or consistent are your limits?	No one listens to me. I nag and yell.	My children know the rules but I forget to enforce them.	My children follow the rules.
12. Do you have reading and math skills?	Minimal skills; low confidence.	Some skills; average confidence.	Strong skills; high confidence.
13. How effective are you as your teenager's teacher?	We always end up fighting.	Sometimes it works, sometimes it doesn't.	It's not easy, but we work together.

Choosing Your Role by Interpreting Your Survey Responses

While there are no hard and fast rules to use in choosing a role, your answers to the survey questions will help you select your role in a systematic way. Using your survey responses, you can use the following guidelines to identify which roles to try first. Remember that any combination of roles is good. To help clarify:

- **The roles of buyer, advocate, and supporter** are appropriate if a majority of your answers fall in the low or medium columns. These roles demand the least amount of direct parent-as-teacher involvement, yet are an important part of test preparation. Most parents can assume these roles.

- **The roles of helper, organizer, and manager** require that the majority of your answers fall in the medium or high columns. These roles involve more constant and direct interaction with your teen. Some parents can assume these roles.

- **The role of tutor** is the most demanding role and requires that at least eleven out of thirteen responses fall in the medium or high columns. There are few parents who can comfortably and successfully assume this role.

Depending on your time and resources, you may, for example, want to begin in the advocate and supporter roles, followed by that of a buyer. If necessary, you could find someone else to act as a manager and tutor. Or, alternatively, you might find yourself best suited to being an organizer, manager, helper, and supporter right away.

Remember that you have flexibility within each role and that roles may change as test preparations move forward. You may switch roles by choice because of unforeseen circumstances. For example, your school may start an SAT prep course, you may change the type of work you do, or your teenager may assume greater responsibility because he selects a particular college and becomes more motivated. Any of these situations may call for a change in your role.

BECOMING ACTIVE

Parents entrust their most valuable assets—their children—to the schools. As an investor in your child's education, you have the same concerns as any other person investing in the future. Unfortunately, sometimes parents are made to feel that the school is the "expert." In some schools, parents are viewed as meddlers if they ask for, or insist upon, information about their children's progress. As a parent, you can, and should, be involved in your teen's education, even at the secondary level. Don't be afraid to pursue information on your teen's behalf—you need to be informed, you need to ask questions, you need to offer suggestions, and you need to reject suggestions if they aren't the right solutions to the problems!

After choosing the roles you will play in your teen's SAT or ACT preparation, you can then focus on the needs of your teenager, while continuing to develop the plan of action that is best for both of you. In the next chapter, we will outline what you need to know about knowing your teen.

MORE RESOURCES: ADVICE FOR PARENTS AND TEENAGERS

Bradley, M. J. & Giedd, J. N. *Yes, Your Teen Is Crazy: Loving Your Kid without Losing Your Mind.* Gig Harbor, WA: Harbor Press, 2003.

Davitz, L. J. & Davits, J. R. *Parenting Teenagers: 20 Tough Questions and Answers.* Mahwah, NJ: Paulist Press, 2003.

Levine, M. *A Mind at a Time.* New York: Simon & Schuster, 2003.

Nelsen, J. & Lott. L. *Positive Discipline for Teenagers: Empowering Your Teens and Yourself through Kind and Firm Parenting.* New York: Random House, 2000.

Rosemond, J. *Teen-Proofing. Fostering Responsible Decision Making in Your Teenager.* Kansas City, MO: Andrews McMeel Publishing, 2001.

Vedrol, J. L. *My Teen Is Driving Me Crazy: A Guide to Getting You and Your Teen through These Difficult Years.* Avon, MA: Adams Media Corporation, 2003.

Waler. S. A. *The Survival Guide for Parents of Gifted Kids: How to Understand, Live with, and Stand up for Your Gifted Child.* Minneapolis, MN: Free Sprit Publishing, 2002.

CHAPTER 3
Knowing Your Teen

HOW TO APPROACH YOUR TEENAGER

Many parents get nervous about the onset of adolescence and associate the teen years with intense experiences, such as being rejected, being in and out of love, having acne, and fighting with "authority" over grades, curfews, friends, or a messy room.

Adolescents do, of course, go through many dramatic changes. For the first time, your teen may be striving for independence and questioning herself and the future. These changes may make your role as a parent additionally tough and you may find it hard to help your teen prepare for college-admissions tests.

The key to reaching your teen is to focus on where he is academically and personally. In this chapter, you'll accomplish the next step of your plan for preparing your teen for the SAT or ACT. This crucial step involves assessing your teen's situation, including his strengths and weaknesses, in preparing for college.

GETTING INFORMATION FROM DIFFERENT SOURCES

To design your SAT or ACT preparation plan, you'll need to get up-to-date information about your teenager from several sources, including yourself, your teenager, and the school. Your child's guidance counselor is a primary source of information, since he can provide information from classroom teachers and across various subject areas.

You and Your Teen

The first source of information is you. Parents must neither overestimate nor underestimate the importance of their own information about their teenager. You can be most effective if you know which questions to ask and whom to ask. You need to know about your teenager's concerns, goals, attitudes, academics, work habits, general behavior, and special strengths and weaknesses.

To initiate this step, ask your teen to meet with you for an hour to discuss his college plans and how he feels about preparing for the SAT or ACT. You can begin by asking your teen for his opinions on matters concerning his education and future goals. In this first conversation, you can ask about colleges he's considering. As many colleges suggest that its applicants' test scores fall within a certain range, information about the college's requirements is important. The required scores may affect the amount of time and the kind of commitment required for SAT or ACT preparation.

You may also want to ask your teen to evaluate his study skills and the kind of study skills needed to prepare for the SAT or ACT. Some teenagers work effectively in groups. Others are uncomfortable or distracted when studying in a group. Students' work habits and interactions with other people also influence their attitudes toward college-admissions tests and toward their scores. Your teenager's reaction to tests in general is an important factor to take into consideration.

Taking the SAT or ACT can create a lot of stress. Excessive anxiety interferes with test performance on the SAT or ACT. Collecting information from your teenager will help identify her problems and concerns, so you can help reduce test-prep stress.

Don't feel rejected if your teen says, "I don't want to meet. I know what to do." Don't push it, just try again later. The timing may be right on the second go-around.

The School

Another important source of information is the school. Guidance counselors, teachers, and others, such as coaches or band directors, can tell you about your teenager's attitudes and interactions with peers and adults outside the home. These attitudes may influence your teen's college selection and in turn lead you to the most appropriate type of preparation for the college-admissions tests.

Your teen's guidance counselor can review previous standardized test scores with you and discuss differences in performance between tests and grades. Reviewing standardized test scores and grades can help you establish realistic guidelines for SAT or ACT preparation.

Teachers and counselors can also describe specific weaknesses that might block an otherwise solid test performance. In addition, they can offer information about your child's work habits, such as whether homework is submitted on time or how well-organized her papers are.

Additional Options

Independent school counselors, or educational consultants, are another alternative to consider. These types of counselors are not affiliated with a school and work as private consultants. If you lack confidence in your teen's counselor or feel that the counselor is too busy to provide the extensive work necessary for appropriate college planning, you may want to work with an educational consultant.

A private consultant may work with students from all over the United States and foreign countries. This broader perspective can provide more diverse options for your child. Many independent counselors also have firsthand experience as college-admissions officers, and therefore are aware of the kind of information that should be collected and ways of presenting such information to colleges.

WHAT TO ASK

The following shows a list of questions you'll want to ask yourself, your teen, and school personnel or educational consultants.

GOALS

- ⌃ What career choices have been considered?
- ⌃ Have specific colleges been identified?
- ⌃ What is the range of SAT or ACT scores considered by those colleges?

ATTITUDES

- ⌃ How positive are feelings toward the ability to succeed?
- ⌃ What attitudes exist toward school and school personnel?
- ⌃ Are current friends a good influence in terms of future plans?
- ⌃ How helpful is the family in terms of school success?
- ⌃ What attitudes exist toward the SAT or ACT?

ACADEMICS

- ⌃ What have other standardized tests shown?
- ⌃ Do standardized test scores accurately reflect skills or abilities?
- ⌃ Do grades accurately reflect skills or abilities?
- ⌃ What are the student's areas of strength?
- ⌃ What are the student's areas of weakness?

WORK HABITS

- ⌃ How effective are organizational and study skills?
- ⌃ Are there preferred study procedures (e.g., groups or tape-recorded lectures)?
- ⌃ How effective are test-taking skills?
- ⌃ Are there problems that might interfere with effective test preparation (e.g., job or extracurricular activities)?
- ⌃ Are there problems that might interfere with effective test-taking (e.g., hates multiple choice, poor at analogies)?

BEHAVIOR

- To what degree does the teenager need or accept help?
- To what degree is the teenager a good decision-maker?
- To what degree is the teenager a self-starter or self-manager?
- To what degree are limits or rules tested?
- How well does the teenager cope with stress or adversity?
- How good are relationships with school personnel?
- How good are relationships with other teenagers?
- How good are relationships with family members?
- With whom does the teenager talk about problems (e.g., brother or neighbor)?

SPECIAL ISSUES

- Are there special talents or strengths?
- Are there special or extraordinary problems?
- Have these issues been addressed previously?
- In what ways will these issues affect SAT or ACT preparation or test-taking?

SAT AND/OR ACT

- How do students in our school perform on the SAT or ACT?
- How did the teenager perform on other college-admissions tests?
- How do test scores compare with others in the class?
- How do test scores compare with others nationally?
- How have other students prepared for the SAT or ACT?
- What services do school personnel provide for SAT or ACT preparation?
- What remedial services are available within the school?
- What remedial or preparatory services are available within the community (e.g., tutors or courses)?

By asking these questions, you can really focus on your teenager. By answering these questions now, you'll reveal information gaps, identify consistencies or inconsistencies in opinions or behaviors, highlight strengths and weaknesses, and begin your systematic plan for helping your teen.

HOW TO USE THE INFORMATION

To get the most out of the information you have collected, pay particular attention to the following issues:

- **Consistency of answers provided by each of the sources**—for example, whether the counselor's answers conflict with your teenager's answers

- **Trends that emerge**—such as better work this year or more anxiety than last year

- **Gaps in information**—such as no previous standardized test scores available

- **Strengths and weaknesses**—such as being well-organized or having poor reading comprehension

The most important aspect to consider when reviewing information is the identification of strengths and weaknesses, since these qualities directly impact how you design an effective SAT or ACT preparation plan.

YOUR TEEN'S STRENGTHS

All teenagers have strengths. However, some teenager's strengths are more obvious than others, and often, when teenagers are difficult, it's hard to think of them in a positive light. Your job as a parent includes:

- Identifying, highlighting, maintaining, and increasing existing strengths

- Providing opportunities for new strengths to develop

Strengths may be grouped into several broad categories—knowledge, work habits, attitude, behavior, and special. To help clarify:

- ◌ **Strengths in the knowledge area** include mastering basic skills, achieving good grades, and having a potential for learning.

- ◌ **Strengths in the area of work habits** include applying skills and knowledge in an organized and effective way and achieving desired goals.

- ◌ **Strengths in the area of attitude** include having clear goals, optimism, motivation, and self-confidence.

- ◌ **Strengths in the behavior category** refer to the teenager's ability to cope, follow home and community rules, and get along with peers and adults.

- ◌ **Special strengths,** for example, include the teenager's talents in the areas of music, writing, or science.

Too frequently, both parents and teachers forget to accent the positive. They zero in on the weaknesses rather than on the strengths. To avoid this common mistake, review the information you have collected and list your teen's strengths and special talents in the following chart. Don't worry; we'll come back to filling in the problem areas later in this chapter.

SOURCE		KNOWLEDGE	WORK HABITS	ATTITUDE	BEHAVIOR	SPECIAL
Parent	Strength					
	Problem					
Teenager	Strength					
	Problem					
School	Strength					
	Problem					

Remember to discuss these strengths with your teenager, especially if he does not recognize his own strengths or talents. Building your teen's confidence is important and will pay off enormously.

IDENTIFYING SPECIFIC PROBLEM AREAS

Several kinds of problems may become obvious as you collect information about your teenager. These problem areas may be grouped into the same five categories we used to identify strengths.

Knowledge Problems

Students with knowledge problems may make statements such as: "I'm not even sure about getting all the ratio and proportion problems right," or "I hate reading," or "I never do those vocabulary parts—I skip most of them."

Knowledge problems include:

- Lack of mastery of basic skills, such as arithmetic
- Lack of understanding of rules and concepts in more advanced areas, such as geometry
- Lack of experience, which leaves gaps in some areas covered on the SAT or ACT
- Difficulties in one or more of the following: remembering previously learned material, analyzing material, or putting information together (e.g., as in a report)

Your teenager may have a knowledge problem in only one area, which may or may not have an effect on any other area. For example, Marcus, a 10th-grader, had a reading problem and testing showed that he read two years below his present grade level. His computation skills were good, and he did well in Algebra. However, word problems were his downfall. In this case, a knowledge problem in one area had an effect on another area.

Improving Memory

Many teenagers complain that they can't remember what they've learned. They make comments such as, "I always forget" or "I studied, but I can't remember." Just as body muscles can be strengthened with practice, memory skills can be improved with exercise and special strategies.

Repeating information aloud and writing facts without looking are active learning techniques that increase the chances of material being remembered. Other techniques for improving memory are:

- **Organize** information into meaningful categories.
- **Find** some way of making the material interesting.
- **Relate** new learning with information already learned.
- **Focus** attention intensely for a short time.
- **Learn** only small amounts of information at any one time.
- **Review** the information frequently.
- **Imagine** the material without actually looking at it.

Work-Habits Problems

Typical work-habits problems statements are: "I can't find my notes," or "I guess I left my books at school," or "I simply cannot do those sentence-completion things!"

Work-habits problems include:

- Poor study habits
- Test anxiety
- Ineffective test-taking skills
- Lack of organization

Teenagers with work-habits problems lack the skills necessary to study effectively or to apply the knowledge they have during a testing situation. These teenagers may work too slowly and be unable to complete portions of the test, or they may work too quickly and inadvertently skip questions and make careless errors.

Attitude Problems

Students with attitude problems may make statements such as: "It doesn't matter how much I study, I'll never be able to do it," or "I don't care—the SAT doesn't matter anyway."

Attitude problems involve:

- Unrealistic self-image and academic goals
- Over- or under-estimation of the importance of the SAT or ACT

On the one hand, teenagers may be overly optimistic in thinking that they are smart, do not need to prepare for the SAT or ACT, and can get into any college on the basis of grades alone. On the other hand, teenagers may have an overly negative view of their ability and therefore avoid school, worry about grades, panic on tests, and be difficult or quarrelsome.

Attitude problems can influence the degree to which teenagers are willing to spend time and energy preparing for the SAT or ACT.

Behavior Problems

Teenagers with behavior problems are likely to make statements such as: "I don't have to study just because you say so," or "I know I should study, but I just can't make myself do it," or "I keep getting headaches when I think about the ACT."

Behavior problems include:

- Poor self-control
- Lack of responsible behavior

- Inability to get along with peers, adults, or family
- Inability or unwillingness to follow rules and maintain commitments in school and in the community
- Drug and/or alcohol abuse

Teenagers with behavior problems usually use ineffective ways of coping with stress, are overly dependent or rebellious, are unable to control anger, and are unwilling to face or discuss problems with adults.

Special Problems

Teenagers with special problems may make statements such as: "I always had trouble with spelling and reading," or "I know I have physical problems, but I want to try to go to college," or "I can do those questions, I just need more time."

Special problems include:

- Specific learning disabilities
- Severe physical, sensory, or emotional limitations
- Dramatically different cultural backgrounds

Other special problems include the language difficulties experienced by some bilingual students or a lack of culturally enriching experiences, which can hamper teenagers from disadvantaged backgrounds.

To begin designing an SAT or ACT plan, you need to review your teenager's problems. List these problems on the same chart where you have already listed the teenager's strengths (see page 41). When discussing these problems with your teenager, remember to talk about his strengths as well.

HOW TO USE THE INFORMATION ABOUT YOUR TEEN

After collecting information about your teenager, you should summarize the information by reviewing the chart you completed. Remember that strengths, along with weaknesses, may exist in each area. Keep the following in mind as you evaluate and summarize the information you have gathered:

- The number of sources that agree or disagree
- The number of objective measures that agree or disagree, such as tests, grades, or reports
- The number of times you are aware of the strength or problem, for example, your teenager always studying or always complaining

Summarizing the Information: One Example

Here's an example of how to use this process. Mr. and Mrs. Coppella completed the questionnaire and were confused. As they looked at the answers to the questions, different impressions came through about their daughter, Grace.

All three sources agreed that Grace was well liked by peers and adults. She put forth a lot of effort with activities in which she was highly interested, such as playing with the band. Her grades were average and she was not taking any honors or Advanced Placement courses. Her standardized test scores were above average, but her vocabulary scores were low. There was a general agreement that if her work habits improved, so would her grades. Grace's work was frequently messy or incomplete, but it was turned in on time. She planned to attend college and felt confident that she would be admitted. Grace's attitude toward the SAT was that it was "no big deal."

When Grace's parents summarized this information, they saw that she had both strengths and weaknesses in the attitude area. Although she felt good about herself, wanted to go to college, and had clear goals, she had an unrealistic view of the importance of the SAT.

The next step for the Coppellas is to match Grace's problems with possible solutions. In the next chapter, we will discuss several approaches parents can use to help their teenagers overcome test-taking problems related to the college-admissions tests.

WORKING WITH YOUR TEEN'S GUIDANCE COUNSELOR

Relative to college-admissions tests, the counselor's role is to help students understand the nature of these tests, the benefits of study and coaching, what test to take and when, and whether to retake a test in order to achieve a higher score.

The counselor can help you and your teen summarize information about how prepared your teen is for the SAT or ACT and can discuss strengths and weaknesses in light of current and past test results and grades. Making an appointment with your teen's counselor now will enable you to make reasonable decisions about a course of action.

A Few Words on Practice Tests

GETTING PERSPECTIVE

This book is designed to help you find a comfortable role to play in your teen's college-admissions test preparation process. The word *comfort* is stressed, because parents often find working with their teen challenging, as adolescence is an age in which unpredictable behavior and struggles for independence are the norm. The test-prep process can also be complicated by the fact that it is the teenager's responsibility to take the SAT or ACT, but usually it's the parent who has the resources and the foresight to get the ball rolling.

As a parent, you understand both the short- and long-term difficulties associated with inadequate and inappropriate planning. So far, you have considered your own roles and collected information to help pinpoint your teenager's strengths and problem areas regarding the SAT or ACT. In Chapters 4 through 8, we'll discuss exactly how to resolve each type of problem: knowledge, work habits, attitude, behavior, and special needs. But before tackling exactly how to minimize or eliminate those problems, let's take a pit stop to help you help your teen find out how he performs on the SAT or ACT right now.

PRACTICE IMPROVES PERFORMANCE

Why have your teen take a practice test now? Taking a practice test will tell both of you more about the areas in which he's doing fine and the areas in which improvement is needed. Taking a practice test now will help you develop a clear, systematic plan that:

⊙ Provides an overview of the training sequence for test-prep

⊙ Identifies strengths and weaknesses

⊙ Offers opportunities for regular practice and coaching

Training isn't based on talk or good intentions alone. Can you imagine an Olympic swimmer only talking about which strokes to practice? Of course not! The swimmer's coach watches the performance and analyzes each of its component parts so that the swimmer can improve on her strengths and overcome her weaknesses. The same procedure can and should be applied to your teen's testing performance.

Making Use of Practice Tests

In working through this chapter, you'll follow a three-step approach to help you and your teen identify and solve performance problems that are specifically related to taking the SAT or ACT.

ANALYZING SAT OR ACT PERFORMANCE PROBLEMS		
STEP 1 Identify the Performance Task	**STEP 2** Identify the Strengths and Weaknesses	**STEP 3** Identify the Training Requirements
☐ What is the SAT or ACT? ☐ How is the test used? ☐ What kinds of tasks does the test require?	☐ What is the current performance level? ☐ Are there patterns in the test results? ☐ What are the teen's test-taking habits and feelings?	☐ What training is necessary? ☐ How long a training period is necessary? ☐ What resources are available?

You may find it useful to ask teachers or other school personnel to become involved in this process.

Step 1: Identify the Performance Task

At this point, your teen needs to know the basic facts about the SAT or ACT. He should be able to answer three questions:

- What is the SAT or ACT?
- Who uses it and how do they use it?
- What kinds of tasks are on the test?

The answers to these questions are readily available from several sources, including guidance counselors, the College Board and ACT Web sites, books, and computer courses. Many of these resources also provide actual previous tests and answers to the questions, first-hand information about the kinds of questions asked, the way in which the questions are asked, and the amount of time allowed for each subtest. Check out the "Appendix A" and "Appendix B" at the back of this book for sample SAT and ACT questions. And don't forget, you can always go back to Chapter 1 of this book for review.

Step 2: Identify the Strengths and Weaknesses

The best way to accurately identify how your teenager will do on the test is to have her take a practice test under conditions that are similar to the administration of the actual test. So, plan a specific time for your teen to take the practice test. By scheduling a time to do this, you stress the importance of becoming oriented to the test.

After taking a practice test, have your teen correct and score her test. This process will provide general scores (e.g., math, writing, and critical reading sections), subtest scores (e.g., reading comprehension), and item analysis. By going through these steps, you and your teen will gain increasingly detailed information about her performance. And by analyzing the results, you can pinpoint her test-taking strengths and weaknesses.

General Scores

The general scores indicate how your teenager's performance compares with other students' scores nationally. Pay attention to differences of more than 30 points between the math and verbal sections. These scores will tell you the basic areas on which your teen needs to focus his preparation. Then review the following general questions with your teen:

- Are these scores consistent with your grades or other standardized tests?
- Did you understand the directions?
- How do you feel about your test performance?

Subtest Scores

When looking at the subtest scores, note any differences between the scores, the highs and lows, or any special trends. At this point, specific problems can be identified. For example, your teen may have correctly answered the majority of the mathematical questions, but when you analyze her test answers, it may become obvious that solving algebra problems is a trouble spot.

Item Analysis

An item analysis is a close examination of the answer that was given for each question. Analyzing items can yield a tremendous amount of useful information. For example, if a student tires easily or works at a very slow pace, most answers will be completed, or more accurate, at the beginning of a subtest. However, if a student works very rapidly, but inaccurately, all the questions may be completed, but there will be many incorrect answers scattered throughout the subtest.

A review of subtest scores without an analysis of individual questions and their answers is misleading and does not provide for systematic test preparation. Although an SAT or ACT score may indicate that further study is needed, only an analysis of the test items will reveal the kind of work that is required in order to increase the scores.

Step 3: Identify the Training Requirements

In order to identify training requirements, you need to establish priorities by:

- ⊙ Reviewing the test and pinpointing the skills that are required by different types of questions
- ⊙ Ranking the subtests in the order of how well your teen fared on each subtest, beginning with the subtest completed most successfully

Ranking the subtest scores shows which areas need the most work. While reviewing the tests for skills, you'll notice certain patterns. For example, in the multiple-choice Writing section of the SAT, similar items are grouped together. In the Critical Reading section, series of reading passages and their corresponding questions are presented with the directions for the section. In the SAT's Mathematics section, questions requiring different kinds of skills, such as logic, estimation, or ratio and proportion, are scattered throughout the test.

Your teenager may need help from you or a teacher to identify question types and the kinds of skills they require.

Pinpointing Areas of Greatest Need

Now you'll want to pinpoint the greatest study needs so that you and your teen can develop a realistic study plan. The amount of time your teenager has available for training before taking the SAT or ACT is a major factor to be considered in test-preparation planning. Of course, the sooner problems are identified, the more training choices you have. For example, if problems are identified after the PSAT performance, then academic courses provided by the school may be used together with other SAT-preparation activities.

Consider the following example. Joan had decided to take only two years of high school mathematics. However, after analyzing her PSAT scores, she realized that there were many problems that she could not answer, as they required more-advanced mathematical knowledge. In addition, she felt that unless her SAT scores were substantially higher than her PSAT scores, the colleges she was considering would not consider her. Analyzing her performance on the PSAT provided Joan with information to use during her junior and senior years. She decided to take a third year of high school mathematics. High school courses were an option Joan could choose, because time was available.

Now consider the case of Greg, who has just decided that he wants to go to college. He took the SAT without preparing for it. After taking the test, he realized that he was not at all prepared for the kinds of questions that were asked and he wasn't used to working under the test's timed conditions. He was unable to finish certain portions of the test. When he received his scores, he was very disappointed. The math scores were consistent with his grades on previous standardized tests. However, the verbal score was much lower than he had anticipated. These scores did not match his grades and previous test scores.

When Greg analyzed his results, he identified two problems: (1) He found that several of the verbal tasks were difficult, and (2) He recognized that he needed to use his time more efficiently while taking the test. Now as a senior applying to college he had to retake the SAT in only six weeks. Given the short time between identifying his problems and retaking the SAT, Greg and his parents decided that the most promising preparation would include special short-term, intensive instruction on test-taking skills. When he practiced his study skills, he focused on the verbal portion of the SAT. To be realistic, Greg and his parents agreed that he had more to gain by learning test-taking skills than by trying to learn one thousand new vocabulary words in less than six weeks.

DON'T LOOSE SIGHT OF YOUR GOAL

Remember that the goal is to increase your teen's SAT or ACT scores. When helping your teen at this crucial point, be careful to avoid three faulty beliefs that parents might come across when faced with the challenge of helping their teen increase their college-admissions test scores. Some parents mistakenly believe that:

- Having discovered the problems, those problems will fade or magically disappear.

- Solutions automatically occur—for example, some parents and teenagers believe that improving study skills alone will immediately result in higher SAT or ACT scores.

- The difficulty of solving test-taking problems is impossible to overcome and effective SAT or ACT preparation is impossible.

It is important to keep in mind that SAT and ACT test-taking problems do have solutions.

To review, your teen will benefit most by:

- Practicing with sample tests
- Identifying the tasks to be performed
- Identifying her individual strengths and weaknesses
- Developing a training plan that is realistic in terms of specific problems and time limits

FINDING YOUR SOLUTIONS

Pinpointing a problem does not automatically correct it. Awareness of a problem without possible solutions can create feelings of anxiety, fear, or helplessness. In response to these feelings, teens may put off action until it's too late or panic and then avoid the situation entirely.

A solution requires careful thought and systematic planning. You and your teenager need to be actively involved in identifying goals, selecting resources, and arranging schedules. The result of an effective solution is a teenager who performs to the best of her ability.

STRATEGIZING YOUR SOLUTIONS

Remember, you are targeting solutions to help your teenager increase his SAT or ACT scores. Improving his work habits is a great goal, but right now, your teen needs to relate that goal to studying for the SAT or ACT.

In creating a plan to help your teen with test-taking skills, consider the following overall goals:

- **Decreasing the problem,** for example, reducing test anxiety
- **Improving skills in weak areas,** for example, improving math skills
- **Using areas of strength,** for example, motivation or positive attitude
- **Managing interfering behaviors,** such as poor organization
- **Dealing with special problems,** such as time limits for teens with disabilities

As a parent, you probably recognize that solutions vary according to the nature and difficulty of the problem. Problems that are long-standing and complicated require more time, energy, and/or money than those that come to light as a result of taking a practice SAT or ACT test. As with all problems, solutions that offer positive effects often require time, patience, commitment, and discipline. In the next few chapters, we'll discuss exactly how to tackle each type of challenge your teen may be facing.

CHAPTER 4

Developing Effective Work Habits

In addition to assessing knowledge of English, math, and other content areas, the SAT and ACT test how well your teen takes standardized tests. Part of becoming a successful test-taker involves developing effective work habits. Developing these habits now will save your teen lots of frustration, time, and energy and will inevitably improve her test scores. In this chapter, we will discuss the habits your teen should develop, including:

   ᕦ Managing time during tests

   ᕦ Organizing study time

   ᕦ Sticking to tasks

We will also outline how you, as a parent, can help your child put these work habits in place, and we'll present possible problem scenarios and solutions.

Recall the survey in Chapter 3. If your teenager showed a need for improvement in the area of work habits, this chapter will be especially helpful for you.

MANAGING TIME

Consider the following example. John is a fairly good student and earns Bs and Cs in his high school courses. He is concerned about the ACT and wants to do well. During a practice ACT test, he plods through each section and spends extra time on some of the more difficult questions. He doesn't finish parts of the test. His practice ACT scores are unnecessarily low because he didn't have time to answer all of the questions he could have easily handled. John's test behavior indicates that he needs help in work habits, especially in learning to manage his time, or pace himself, during the test.

When people work in factories or offices, they are usually told how much time should be spent on different tasks. This process ensures productivity, allowing workers to know what is expected of them and helping them pace themselves so that they get the most done in the least amount of time. Similarly, your teen will also benefit from learning how to manage the time he has to take the SAT or ACT. Before taking the tests, he should know the following:

- How many questions are on each section of the test

- How much time is provided for each section

- Approximately how much time can be given to each question if he is to complete the test and if all of the questions are of equal difficulty

- The kinds of questions that he can't do and should skip until he has completed those questions he can definitely answer correctly

With test-taking, managing time means that your teen can predict what she has to do, how long it should take, how to pace herself to get the job done, and how to leave time to check her work. Although most testing centers have clocks, your teen should wear a watch during the test (and practice tests) to keep track of time and check her pacing.

GETTING ORGANIZED AND STICKING TO TASKS

Now consider the case of another test-taker, Vera. The following takes place in her parents' kitchen after dinner:

7:05 p.m. "Mom, did you see my SAT practice book?"

7:10 p.m. "Mom, I found some paper. Where are some pencils?"

7:15 p.m. "Oh, I'd better call Nien to see if I have a ride tomorrow!"

7:20 p.m. "What time is it?"

7:22 p.m. "I need to get on the computer."

7:25 p.m. "That's enough math! I think I'll do some vocabulary."

7:40 p.m. "I hate vocabulary! I'll go back to math."

Vera displays several work-habits problems. One problem is that she hasn't recognized what she can't do during study time—for example, disrupting herself by making phone calls. Another problem is that Vera jumps from task to task, breaking her own concentration.

Good work habits entail being organized. Teenagers need to learn how to organize materials, list what has to be done, and specify how much time might be needed to complete each job. Study styles may differ, but teenagers must find the most effective ways to use their time and follow their own plans.

Students like Vera benefit from guidelines to follow during study time, such as the ones following:

⊙ Spend at least 20–30 minutes on each activity, maintaining concentration, and building up skills.

⊙ Stick to some basic study rules, including not avoiding work because it is too difficult or boring.

⊙ Invoke the rule: "Work first and then play." For example, make phone calls only after work is completed.

Sticking to a task is an essential work habit. Unless she changes her habits, Vera will not reach the critical test-related goal: accurately completing the greatest number of problems she can within specific time limits. Vera is also operating under some misconceptions. She really believes that she is working hard and that her fatigue is a result of studying. She may also begin to think that she is not as bright as her friends because they are getting better results on practice tests. All of these potential problems can be resolved by changing her work habits.

If It Works, Don't Change It

Another 10th grader, Ralph, likes his comforts. He loads up on soda and chips before he settles down to work. The radio is an essential part of his lifestyle. When his mother and sisters pass by his room, they see him sprawled on his bed with a small light turned on and papers and books all over the floor. Sometimes he's sound asleep. Because he seems so casual, everybody stops by and talks to him.

Some parents might assume that the manner in which Ralph goes about studying is totally ineffective. It doesn't appear that any teenager could concentrate and maintain attention curled up in bed, with music blaring, people walking in and out, poor lighting, and a nap here and there. Most parents would be right. Ralph's parents had been concerned and were annoyed by his work habits. However, Ralph earns high grades in school and on the first SAT he took, he scored more than 600 on both the Verbal and the Mathematic sections. He has also shown his parents how his speed is increasing on certain practice SAT exercises. In this case, the parents have specific information and assurance that although his work habits appear inefficient, they happen to work for their teenager.

Your objective here is to check the effectiveness of your teenager's work habits. Consider what effect these habits have on classroom or college-admissions test performance. Remember to have your teen take a practice test under actual SAT or ACT conditions to see how his work habits hold up.

TAMING THE PROCRASTINATOR

Procrastination is a common problem for teens. Leslie is an 11th-grader having a conversation with her father, Mr. Rand.

Mr. Rand: "Did you start to study for the ACT?"

Leslie: "No, it's in two months."

Mr. Rand: "Shouldn't you start now?"

Leslie: "I wish you would stop nagging me. I can take care of myself."

Here's another scenario, between Mrs. Sanchez and her 11th-grader, Ricky:

Mrs. Sanchez: "I haven't seen that SAT book around. Are you studying in school?"

Ricky: "I started looking at it, and it's so long I'll never get through it."

Putting off work occurs when teenagers feel overwhelmed, don't know where to begin, feel pressured to get other things done, or are distracted by other things they would rather do. Parents who recognize this work-habits problem in their teenagers may have similar habits themselves.

Procrastination becomes a particular problem because:

- ◌ Time is limited; when time is limited, people feel pressure.
- ◌ There can be a penalty for delay—for example, when you miss the SAT or ACT because your check was mailed late.
- ◌ Avoiding work increases the load, rather than decreases it.

By taking into account the time available before the SAT or ACT and the preparation that has to be done, you can help your teenager create a sensible plan that reduces one seemingly overwhelming task to many smaller and more manageable ones. Predicting what has to be done, and doing those tasks one by one, gives teenagers control over feelings of being swamped and unable to cope.

A WORK-HABITS CHECKLIST

To help your teenager develop effective work habits, ask him questions regarding time management, materials, atmosphere, and space. You may want to use the following checklist.

TIME MANAGEMENT

☐ Are there signals to others that this is a study time (e.g., a "Do Not Disturb" sign)?

☐ Are there rules set up for the study time (e.g., no phone calls or no visitors)?

☐ Is a time schedule agreed upon and posted?

☐ Are study breaks scheduled?

MATERIALS

☐ Is a clock or kitchen timer available?

☐ Are supplies handy (e.g., pencils, eraser, computer)?

☐ Does the seating encourage attention and alert behavior (e.g., a chair and a desk rather than a bed)?

ATMOSPHERE

☐ Is the lighting adequate?

☐ Is the noise level low?

☐ Is the area visually non-distracting?

☐ Is the area well-ventilated and does it have a moderate temperature?

SPACE

☐ Is there a special place designated (e.g., desk, room, or area)?

☐ Is this space away from the main traffic of the home?

☐ Is the space large enough to allow for writing?

☐ Is there space available for storing or filing materials?

HOW TO HELP YOUR TEEN WITH WORK HABITS

Teenagers have difficulty finding time to do homework or household chores, but they usually seem to have a lot of time to talk on the phone and meet with friends. Managing time comes down to establishing priorities. Here are some guidelines that you can use to help your teenager use her time more effectively:

- Set a realistic study schedule that doesn't interfere too much with normal activities.

- Divide the task into small and manageable parts—for example, instead of trying to memorize two-thousand vocabulary words in two weeks, have your teen learn and use five new words a day, three times a week.

- Use what has just been learned whenever it is possible—for example, talk about, joke about, and use new or obscure vocabulary words.

- Find times that are best for concentration and, if possible, have your teen avoid studying at times when she is tired, hungry, or irritable.

- Plan a variety of study breaks, such as music or jogging, to revive concentration.

Using Study Groups

You may also want to encourage your teenager to get a group of friends together to practice taking the SAT or ACT, review test items, compare answers, and/or discuss the ways they used to solve the problems. Such a group can range in size from two to six students.

Consider this example: Ms. Franklin realized that her daughter, Barbara, liked to be with other teenagers and studied best in a group. If she waited for Barbara to begin studying independently, Ms. Franklin was afraid that Barbara would put off studying until it was too late.

Ms. Franklin asked her daughter if she would like to organize a study group. Ms. Franklin also volunteered to provide the house and find a tutor. Barbara's responsibilities were to call her friends, tell them which materials to buy, how much each session would cost, and where and when the group would meet. By doing this, Ms. Franklin provided a real service to a group of motivated students who needed some direction.

So, if you want to help set up a study group, you can:

- Make the initial arrangements
- Provide the space for meetings
- Set up a "study atmosphere" in your home
- Help other parents to set up such groups

Your Role: More Tips on Organization

When reading about Ms. Franklin, you might think that she is very organized and efficient. Nope! In fact, she is usually disorganized and is a procrastinator herself. She rarely plans ahead, and there is a lot of confusion in her home when deadlines must be met. She and her husband even had to drive to several colleges to deliver Barbara's college applications so that they arrived on time.

Ms. Franklin's behavior shows that it really is possible for an otherwise hassled parent to become more organized and efficient for a short time just for the SAT or ACT. During this brief window, you can help your teen by doing the following:

- Save papers and announcements with dates and requirements for the SAT or ACT.
- Make copies of all correspondence, applications, checks, and bills and find one place to store or file these papers.
- Write the SAT and/or ACT date and your teenager's study-session schedule on your own calendar.
- Write notes to yourself so that you don't forget to do what you said you'd do, such as making phone calls or picking up materials.

MORE WORK-HABITS SCENARIOS: PROBLEMS AND SOLUTIONS

Here are some brief scenarios presenting work-habits problems and possible remedies.

Scenario 1

Your son comes home and goes directly to the refrigerator, stating that he is tired from soccer practice. He says, "I better get going, I have to read that SAT review book."

You say, "You seem tired. Perhaps you ought to eat, rest a little, and *then* study when you have more energy."

Scenario 2

Your daughter is carrying around reams of papers containing exercises for every kind of math problem on the ACT. She's exhausted and hassled.

You say, "What about studying one kind of problem at a time and then moving on to the next type?" *Or* "Why don't you practice only one kind of problem this week?"

Scenario 3

Your son scored 525 on the Verbal and 379 on the Mathematics sections of the PSAT. You see him practicing reading exercises.

You say, "Which do you think is more important, raising your verbal or your math score?"

In these situations, parents recognize problems, make suggestions, and try to help the teenager correct the problem on his own. Notice that the parents ask questions rather than criticizing or telling the teenager what to do.

Teens will be more receptive to advice when it is offered in a manner that appears to give them choices.

LIFE DURING THE COLLEGE-ADMISSIONS TEST PROCESS

Believe it or not, family life goes on in spite of the SAT or ACT. Teenagers really do survive college-admissions tests and go on to college. In the interim, however, teenagers are frequently irritable, dump their problems on other family members, and create tension in the home. Parents who are trying to help often get angry when they feel that their efforts are not recognized or appreciated. Here are some helpful hints for those times when things seem to be getting out of control:

- Don't take on more than you can reasonably handle.

- When the going gets tough, remember the good things you did and are trying to do.

- Take a walk, call a friend, or go to the movies. In other words, relax and enjoy yourself.

- Most important, remember that you will survive—this is especially important if you have other children who will be taking the SAT or ACT at a later date!

CHAPTER 5
Fixing Knowledge Problems

Many of the challenges teenagers face on the SAT or ACT are the result of knowledge problems. In other words, some students need to gain knowledge of math, English, writing, and/or other content areas in order to improve their scores. There are many ways to help your teen to learn what she needs to know.

THREE APPROACHES

There are three basic approaches to gaining knowledge of specific subjects:

- ⭕ Remedial work
- ⭕ Review work
- ⭕ New learning

Remedial Work

Remedial work consists of improving specific skills in one or more subject areas. This approach should be taken if any one of these four factors exists:

- ⭕ Any standardized test reveals two or more years difference between test scores and present grade level.

- ⭕ The student has earned a C or below in English or math.

- ⭕ The PSAT and/or PLAN scores or practice SAT and/or ACT tests show weakness in a specific area (such as Algebra or reading comprehension) or in a specific skill (such as understanding test directions).

- ⭕ The teenager talks about a lack of skills—for example, he makes statements such as: "I have always been a slow reader," "I need to learn to read faster," or "I hate geometry."

Review Work

Review work assumes the teenager has effective skills in reading, writing, and math. Review ensures that these skills are recalled quickly and are then demonstrated on the SAT or ACT with accuracy and speed.

For example, James has taken three years of math and received Bs in all of his math courses. Early in his senior year he took an ACT practice test. The results showed a need to brush up on his math skills. He is the perfect candidate for a short and intensive ACT review course.

Then there is Danetta, an avid reader who receives As and Bs in her English courses and loves to write. She has a good vocabulary, but rarely has opportunities to apply her vocabulary skills to tasks similar to those tested on the SAT. A review course would familiarize her with SAT-type reading passages and questions.

New Learning

New learning is for those teenagers who were never taught, or who lacked the opportunity to acquire, the skills necessary for the SAT or ACT. For example, Alan took general math and then decided that mathematics was not for him. He never seriously considered going to college until the end of his junior year. His guidance counselor told him that he needed more math study to do well on the ACT and suggested taking Algebra and geometry courses in summer school.

To remedy gaps in knowledge, your teen may want to take courses, work with a tutor, or use another test-prep method. Before discussing specific resources, let's look at the differences between coaching and instruction, as they each refer to different approaches to improving test-taking skills.

The type of solution you choose depends on your teenager's strengths and problem areas, the amount of time he has, and your resources.

WHAT IS COACHING?

Coaching means teaching students to:

- ⊙ Become familiar with the SAT or ACT format
- ⊙ Make effective use of test time
- ⊙ Become aware of general test-taking techniques
- ⊙ Become skilled at applying specific strategies in order to make "educated guesses" at answers
- ⊙ Use practice tests to increase speed and accuracy
- ⊙ Become skilled at managing test-related stress

For example, one important test-taking skill is knowing how and when to guess on multiple-choice questions. When using guessing strategies on questions they don't know the answers to, students reduce the number of choices by eliminating obviously wrong answers. They then make a guess. By reducing the number of choices, test-takers increase their odds of a correct response. Learning guessing strategies is one skill the student gains from coaching.

The purpose of coaching is to help teenagers increase test-taking knowledge and skill so that they become "test-wise." Being test-wise allows them to demonstrate what they already know.

Colleges report seeing students relying more and more on counselors and consultants to prepare them for college-admissions tests. This trend will increase as new tasks and skills, such as essay writing, are added to college-admissions tests.

When Is Coaching Most Effective?

Research suggests that some students more than others benefit from coaching. Coaching helps students who already have verbal and math skills but who experience any one of the following challenges:

- ○ Lack of confidence in their abilities
- ○ Lack of experience with standardized tests
- ○ Lack of familiarity with the format of test items
- ○ Lack of awareness of all the kinds of problems on the math section
- ○ Poor performance on standardized tests in comparison with their grades or their class rank

Many students who enroll in formal coaching programs come from families with a high level of formal education and high income, have higher degree aspirations, have taken many high school courses in math, science, and foreign language, and want to go to the more competitive colleges. Coached students are also likely to engage in multiple test-preparation strategies. They buy more prep books, hire more tutors, and study longer than other students.

WHAT IS INSTRUCTION?

Instruction includes helping students to:

- ○ Improve their vocabulary
- ○ Increase their reading comprehension and rate of reading
- ○ Increase their knowledge and application of mathematical concepts
- ○ Increase their knowledge and understanding in other subject areas, including the social and physical sciences

Instruction entails long-term preparation that is focused on the thinking and knowledge skills that are needed for the reading and math portions of the SAT or ACT. Instruction supports the existing school curriculum, frequently using specially developed materials.

Students who engage in this type of learning have been known to increase their verbal SAT scores by more than 100 points and their math scores by more than 75 points. Instruction materials that can be used to gain such skills are in the "List of Resources."

It should come as no surprise that past and recent research indicate that studying can make a huge difference in improving SAT and ACT scores.

While considering whether coaching, instruction, or both are best suited to your teen's needs, you may want to further investigate options such as courses and tutoring. Let's now look at these offerings in detail.

TYPES OF COURSES

Courses usually provide instruction in a group setting and focus on remedial work, review work, or new learning. Many courses are provided in schools, including:

- Courses in traditional content areas, such as English, science, and math
- Courses specifically designed to improve skills, such as composition, grammar, and reading rate and comprehension
- Remedial courses that increase skill proficiency in areas such as reading, writing, grammar, and math
- Computer-based courses in vocabulary, reading, grammar, and math

School-based courses may be available to help students with the SAT or ACT. Such instruction can focus on a specific SAT or ACT subject area or on general test-taking strategies. These courses may be offered as part of a regular English or math course, as a special short-term course given after school, or as an elective for credit.

In addition to the courses offered at your teen's school, you may want to think about commercially offered courses. These types of courses exist in almost every community and should be considered when:

- The school lacks the resources to provide such courses.
- School personnel are unwilling to provide courses.
- Your teenager needs more or different instruction than the school can reasonably be expected to provide.

For example, Frank desperately needs a crash course to improve his reading comprehension and reading rate before taking the SAT. He has two months to prepare for the test. The school offers a reading course that meets once a week for six months. However, a commercial course that meets twice a week for six weeks is also available. In this situation, a commercial course might be considered, if finances allow.

Jane, on the other hand, experiences difficulty organizing her thoughts in writing. She has good ideas but doesn't take the time to plan before she writes. She often loses points on English reports and tests due to poor organization. Her counselor suggests a tutor who is a retired English teacher. Jane works with the tutor on a weekly basis and improves her composition skills for the writing portion of the SAT. In addition to earning higher scores on the SAT, Jane improves her performance on classroom tests.

Commercial Courses

Commercial SAT and ACT prep courses are advertised in both local and national newspapers and on the Web. Courses range in price from $125 (for an 18-hour intensive weekend course) to $900 (for about 45 hours of test-prep drills and practice tests). Prices vary from region to region.

The people who teach these commercially available courses are college graduates, although they are not usually certified teachers. In order to be hired as teachers, however, they must have taken the SAT or ACT and performed extremely well.

In most commercial courses, students are first given a test to determine their SAT- or ACT-related strengths and weaknesses. Then students are grouped according to their ability. If students are weaker in the verbal area, the first 2 hours of each 4-hour session are spent mastering verbal skills. Those students who are weaker in math have 2 hours of math first. Classes to improve writing skills are also offered. This arrangement allows students to tackle the subject that is harder for them at the time when they are freshest.

Some longer courses include ten 4-hour coaching sessions with assigned homework after each session. Each session starts with a test on what has just been learned and reviewed. In the ninth session students are given a practice test, and their answers are analyzed during the tenth session.

The course may also offer a practice center for additional work after the student is enrolled in the course. In some courses, after taking the SAT, if students are dissatisfied with their scores, they can still use the practice center free of charge to improve their skills before retaking the test.

A Word about Preparing for the Writing Section

Traditionally, students have little practice in writing essays under testing conditions, since most high school students are not required to analyze, organize, write, and edit essays for classroom tests. Although students are required to write long essays and reports in school, they are not required to write them in class under time constraints and without benefit of a computer, spell checker, and perhaps, parental feedback.

The SAT writing section requires the skill of writing under timed conditions. This skill is necessary for college success and should be taught and practiced in high school courses. As a parent, you may have to encourage teachers and school administrators to offer some type of instruction on the SAT or ACT in the schools, especially in relation to the newer Writing and Math sections of the SAT. You should feel justified in making these suggestions since research shows that coaching or studying is most effective when spread over a long period of time and combined with regular school work.

Community-Group Courses

Some community groups also offer test-prep courses. Bilingual teenagers or students from poorer communities may be motivated to participate in an SAT or ACT course when the course is led by a community member and when their friends can also be involved. To help bilingual students become familiar with the SAT or ACT and its format, translating an SAT or ACT practice test into the teenager's native language can be very useful. Removing the language barrier increases the bilingual teenager's confidence in her ability to succeed on the SAT or ACT in English.

DIFFERENT KINDS OF TUTORS

Tutoring usually involves instruction on an individualized basis and focuses on remedial help, review work, or new learning. You might consider tutoring for your teen when:

- Your teenager is uncomfortable in group settings or she learns best in a one-on-one teacher-student situation.

- The tutor has the expertise and experience with SAT or ACT preparation that is not available in school.

- Your teenager has specific needs that would not be appropriately met in a group situation.

- The pace of group instruction would either be too fast or too slow.

There are several different types of tutors. The most easily found tutors are schoolteachers who work outside of school for additional fees. These kinds of tutors are advantageous in that they are familiar with the school curriculum, can identify learning gaps, and are probably familiar with your teen.

Professional tutors are usually certified teachers with experience. They know about standardized testing and can usually interpret test results. They also have access to test-prep materials and either other support personnel if additional information is needed. Professional tutors work independently or are affiliated with a private organization. An advantage of these tutors is that their hours are more flexible. For example, Tommie gets out of school at 1 p.m. She has a job as a waitress from 4 p.m. to 8 p.m. She needs to find a tutor who is available between 1:30 p.m. and 3 p.m., so she decides to work with a professional tutor.

Teenagers are more receptive to instruction and more willing to work when their tutoring sessions are both comfortable and convenient.

Community volunteers also offer their time as tutors through organizations, such as the YMCA, 4-H Club, Community Center, or religious groups. Tutoring by volunteers may be far less expensive than other types of tutoring.

Peer tutors are another option. Peer tutoring means that students who have skills in specific areas act as tutors for other students. An advantage of using a peer tutor for SAT or ACT preparation is that the peer tutor may have just recently taken these tests. Peer tutors who received high scores on the SAT or ACT can identify problems and concerns of their peers and can offer both instruction and coaching in test-taking tips.

With peer tutors, the cost is usually minimal, especially if the tutor receives school credit for his work. Colleges often offer community service opportunities in which college students provide tutoring as part of a course requirement. However, you may want to consider some drawbacks related to peer tutoring. Peer tutors are not certified teachers, and they may lack the experience necessary to be effective. Ask your teen's guidance counselor for help in selecting appropriate peer tutors.

Parents can also act as tutors. In fact, an increasing number of parents are tutoring or home-schooling their own children. Many parents have discovered that tutoring is a skill that can be learned and improved. Some parents learn these skills with ease, while others require practice. As a parent, you may be able to gain tutoring skills at your child's school by volunteering as a teacher's aide.

You may want to assess whether the tutoring role is right for you by looking back at the "Parent Survey" in Chapter 2 (page 31).

Within the role of tutor, you can take on several tasks. The most common activity involves explaining or providing information. This is appropriate for the parent who has knowledge of a particular area, such as Algebra or English. However, there are other less demanding ways in which you can help your teen—remember, you can engage in many different roles! For example, you can organize and arrange materials and equipment, set up a study schedule, keep time, check work, or help monitor progress.

One parent, an ex-teacher, borrowed a series of vocabulary and reading comprehension books from the school, organized a three-teenager study group, set a schedule, and read the instructions into a tape recorder to help the students use the materials. Sometimes she checked the accuracy of the teenagers' work, provided supportive statements, or announced times for study breaks. Since she lacked the funds to hire a tutor or to pay for a course, she set up a study center and acted as the instructional manager.

Elsewhere, a group of parents were short of extra funds. Since their teenagers enjoyed listening to tapes, they pooled their money and jointly purchased commercially prepared vocabulary and mathematics audiotapes.

College-Admission Tests Are a Family and School Affair

Educators have emphasized the importance of parental involvement with SAT and ACT preparation for more than two decades. In its report, Testing for College Admissions: Trends and Issues, the Educational Research Service—an independent, non-profit institution—noted that: "Student and parental attitudes are critical to good SAT scores. . . Schools with stable or rising test scores credit students and parents with high academic aspirations and a commitment to work toward those aspirations."

Remember that whatever role you choose to play during SAT or ACT preparation will help your teen do her best on the tests.

More Tips on Selecting a Tutor

A critical factor when selecting any tutor is the tutor's familiarity with the PSAT, SAT, PLAN, or ACT. Just being skilled in a subject area is usually not enough, as students must be able to apply the knowledge in that area in order to answer the test questions. When selecting a tutor, you should feel free to ask how much experience the tutor has in teaching the test your teen is taking. For the bilingual student, it is essential that the tutor be bilingual in order to determine whether problems are language- or skill-related. You should also consider costs, the time frame, convenience of location, and other factors previously outlined.

INDEPENDENT STUDY

Independent study describes learning that occurs when students teach themselves. Teenagers who are academically skilled, self-motivated, and able to organize their own study time are most likely to profit from independent study.

Consider the case of Sara. Sara is an A student. Her teachers compliment her on her sense of responsibility. She was pleased with her PSAT scores and is very motivated. Sara wants to be sure that she does well on the SAT, so she has set up a weekly study schedule to review Algebra and geometry and practice for the essay sections.

When teenagers study independently, they can use:

- SAT and ACT practice books that explain the test, provide practice exercises and answer keys, and offer study and test-taking tips

- Test-taking books, which center on specific academic or study skills, such as acquiring vocabulary

Many of these materials are available in school reading and math labs and in libraries. Materials for use on computers sometimes can be found in schools or can be purchased for use at home. These materials can be shared by several families to reduce costs.

Depending on your teen's attitudes and habits, he may choose different test-prep activities, such as individual tutoring, a course, or using a test-prep book.

WORKING WITH YOUR TEEN'S GUIDANCE COUNSELOR

When deciding on a type of coaching or instruction, you may want to consult your teen's guidance counselor. Counselors are responsible for understanding different types of knowledge problems and the varied kinds of tutors and/or coaching that are available. In addition, counselors can provide advice about the appropriate match between the student and the available services.

CHAPTER 6

Adjusting Attitudes

GETTING A HANDLE ON ATTITUDE PROBLEMS

Attitude problems are generally more difficult to get a handle on than work-habits or knowledge problems, as attitude problems tend to be less specific. A teenager's attitude problem affects the way he relates to adults, the friends he associates with, and the way he performs in school. Although these attitudes are more difficult to change, you can use several approaches and techniques to positively influence attitudes.

Describe, Don't Label

"Zhu has ability, but her attitude keeps her from getting good grades."

"Simon's poor attitude toward school makes it hard for us to work with him."

If your teen has an attitude problem, you may have heard such statements from his teachers or guidance counselor. Or, you may have found yourself telling your teenager, "If your attitude were better, your grades would be better."

What do these remarks have in common? All of them suggest that something is wrong, but they do not describe what the problem is. When addressing attitude problems, it's a good idea to give specific descriptions of what behavior could be improved.

HONING IN ON ATTITUDES

The following information about attitudes can help you figure out what drives your teen's attitude problem. Attitudes are:

- Usually reactions based on previous experiences

- Emotional feelings, ideas, or beliefs that determine how people will react to future events

- A state of being, ready to respond in a certain way to an event, situation, or person

Attitudes can be positive or negative, mild or intense, and influence the way your teenager responds to people and events on a daily basis. Attitudes also serve several purposes, as they:

- Protect teenagers from facing and accepting things about themselves that may be disappointing or unpleasant

- Help express values

- Help make sense out of a world that is changing, complicated, and confusing

- Provide a sense of predictability when teenagers believe that they have little control over their lives or when their decision-making is limited— for example, the teenager who is constantly late to class, but knows there are consequences for being late

---

Teens may exhibit attitude problems by making statements such as: "I hate English. Ms. Duras says I write like a 1st-grader," "You never learn anything in school," "Going to college doesn't mean making a lot of money," or "No matter what I do, it won't work out. Why should I bother?"

When trying to understand attitude problems, you should consider three factors: private messages, responses, and behavior. Each of these factors influences the other. To illustrate these factors, let's consider the example of Liz, who feels that she is not very bright. Liz's parents have been told that she has ability, but Liz still thinks poorly of herself.

◌ Her **private message,** or secret thought or belief, is "I can't do the work, so I must be stupid."

◌ Her **response,** or feeling, is that she becomes anxious before and during tests to the extent that she does poorly on them.

◌ Her **behavior,** or action, is disinterest in school and not participating in class.

Liz's message, response, and behavior work together to create a cycle in which each factor contributes to and maintains the other factors. When addressing attitude problems, you may want to try to break down the problem by figuring out what your teen's private message is, what her response is, and what behavior results from and perpetuates her thoughts and feelings.

Past experience can create negative attitudes. Some teenagers who feel inadequate set up roadblocks, or defenses, to protect themselves from more negative experiences. Other teenagers make inaccurate or incorrect decisions based on past experiences, which in turn reinforce their feelings of inadequacy.

DOES YOUR TEENAGER HAVE AN ATTITUDE PROBLEM?

It may be difficult to distinguish an attitude problem from the typical concerns of adolescence. Some teenagers and their families breeze through adolescence, but most others do not. The adolescents' sudden mood shifts and their general confusion about the changes in their lives often create tension in the home. And on top of it all, the college-admissions tests occur in the midst of these changes.

Both parents and teenagers who do not recognize the importance of the SAT or ACT, or who have received conflicting information about the tests, have difficulty sorting out their roles and making decisions. Sometimes, teens avoid preparing for the tests to avoid further conflict. The following scenarios shows how confusing situations can become and the negative effect confusion has on SAT or ACT preparation.

Scenario 1

Mr. Allen: "Where's Bob? Doesn't he usually come to these games?"

John: "He's taking an ACT course."

Mr. Allen: "Why aren't you?"

John: "I don't have the time and it's not that important. Besides, no one else is taking it."

Mr. Allen: "It might help. Why do you care what your friends do? Besides, if I am willing to foot the bill you should do it."

John: "You don't even know what the ACT is. You're always so sure you know everything. My counselor makes less of a deal about it than you do."

Mr. Allen: "You're right. If you're lazy and don't care, why should I waste my money?"

Several points are illustrated by this example:

- Peer groups influence decisions.
- The parent's suggestions are given but not heard.
- The teen's present and future goals are unclear.
- This teen, like many others, frequently feels pressured and overwhelmed.
- The school may provide minimal information.
- The teenager and/or parent have inaccurate information about the test.
- The teenager thinks that parents are negative and interfering.
- The parent feels that the teenager is lazy and unappreciative.

Analyzing the Situation

Mr. Allen believes that John is lazy and ungrateful. In other words, he thinks John has an attitude problem. However, Mr. Allen later bumped into Bob's father who said, "First I thought Bob was lazy, but then I found out he knew nothing about the ACT." In this case, as in others, what appeared to be an attitude problem was a teenager's reaction to inadequate or inaccurate information.

What Is the Solution?

For the Allen family, the first step is to get John some information about the ACT and the effect studying can have on test scores. This remedy should avoid further conflict and confusion. The information John needs can be obtained from several sources:

- Bob can tell John what the course is about and why he is taking it.

- Mr. Allen can find articles from newspapers and magazines about the ACT and the effects of coaching, and show them to John.

- Mr. Allen can contact John's guidance counselor and ask him to explain the importance of the ACT to John.

Giving John the information he needs neutralizes the conflicts and enables him to make better decisions about preparing for the test.

Scenario 2

Ellen is a different kind of teenager. She makes many remarks indicating that she has a low opinion of herself, such as: "I never do well in school." Her parents are tired of going to school conferences and hearing comments such as, "Ellen is bright, but she doesn't seem to care." The funny thing is that Ellen talks about going to college. Ellen's unhelpful attitude toward school and herself will probably keep her from even considering SAT preparation. Her parents don't know what else to do. They feel that they have tried everything.

Another Solution

Several different approaches can be used in situations similar to Ellen's. All of these methods try to create a new outlook and a fresh start because situations and events need to present a new picture with a sense of optimism and hope for the teen.

The best thing for parents to do is to indirectly change the teenager's attitude by working around it. They can present new ideas for consideration or just plunge ahead and attempt to change her behavior. Ellen's parents could try any one of the following solutions:

- They could indirectly focus on her future goal of going to college by arranging to get some brochures and/or visiting colleges earlier than they had planned. This action may refocus Ellen's attention on the task at hand.

- Although they have probably discussed her strengths in the past, they could give her even more encouragement. Sometimes, this support can come from other family members, close friends, or clergy.

- They could ignore her negative attitudes toward school and focus on finding a terrific tutor who can direct Ellen's attention to the SAT.

- They might consider having Ellen enroll in a nearby summer college program for teenagers or, if money is available, having her live at a college and attend a specialized program.

- They could be empathetic about her current situation, yet encouraging about the future, by making statements such as, "I know you're turned off by high school, but you seem to be excited about college, and we think you'll do well there," or "Let's try something different just for the SAT."

It's always a good idea to give your teen encouragement. Most teens benefit from supportive statements such as, "You are someone special and I know that this will work out."

The key in this type of situation is to find ways to redirect the student's attention to the immediate goal of preparing for the tests and provide consistent support for this goal.

WORKING WITH YOUR TEEN'S GUIDANCE COUNSELOR

Counselors can help improve teenagers' attitudes about the value of study. They can stress how studying can make a difference on SAT and ACT tests.

Frequently, teenagers with attitude problems will find themselves in the counselor's office. Problems with attitude can result from depression, school failure, and/or family problems. Classroom teachers sometimes refer students to the counselors, who are trained to follow up with students and their parents and, when necessary, to make referrals to other professionals.

If your teen has attitude problems, you should know that the counselor is a valuable resource and make an appointment to meet with him.

CHAPTER 7

Recognizing and Improving Behavior Problems

Teenagers' behaviors reflect their attempts to deal with the world, influence how others deal with them, and the types of decisions that will be made by and about them. Some teenagers have already learned extremely useful ways of reacting to the people and responsibilities in their lives; other teenagers have not yet learned such skills. If your teen finds that developing appropriate behaviors is challenging, your job is to identify the kinds of behavior problems you see, decide the extent to which these problems might influence performance on the SAT or ACT and future career plans, and help your teenager deal with these challenges. Behavior problems do have solutions, and we'll explore them in this chapter.

If you are having trouble determining whether your teen has behavior problems, review the survey you completed in Chapter 3 (page 45).

WHAT IS BEHAVIOR?

When helping your teen improve his behavior, it's good to keep in mind the following points:

- **Behavior is learned**—teenagers' current behaviors result from their past experiences and lessons they previously learned.

- **Behavior can be changed**—the teenage years are the time for trying out, revising, adding, and shedding different kinds of behaviors, especially those which are not appropriate or effective.

- **Behavior is influenced by the people and surroundings in your teenager's life**—parents, school personnel, friends, and experiences affect teen behaviors.

- **Circumstances can be rearranged** to help teenagers change their behavior.

Identifying Behavior Problems

Parents often lump all kinds of behavior problems together, even when there are vast differences. Problems, such as staying out too late, cutting class, and acting like a smart aleck, often require different approaches to modify them. At SAT or ACT time, you need to focus on those problems that present barriers to test preparation or effective test-taking. Your first task is to decide whether a behavior problem is specific just to the home situation, to one area of school learning, or to your teenager's entire school performance.

Use the following questions to help you identify the kinds of behavior problems your teen exhibits:

- Are these behaviors a problem at home?
- Are these behaviors a problem in school?
- Will these behaviors interfere with grades?
- Will these behaviors interfere with test performance?
- Will these behaviors prevent passing from grade to grade?
- Will these behaviors negatively influence his chances for college admission?
- Do these behaviors endanger his health or the safety of others?

Prioritizing Behavior Problems

Once you've identified what type of behavior problems your teen displays, you can prioritize fixing the problems. Some problems can and should be ignored for now, while others should be dealt with promptly and directly. If the problem endangers your teen or the safety of others, you should address the problem immediately. If, on the other hand, the behavior problem does not affect schoolwork or SAT or ACT preparation and presents no immediate danger to the teen or others, the problem can be ignored for the moment.

While you help your teen prepare for the tests, you may want to focus on having her develop effective work habits or gain knowledge, rather than addressing broad behavioral patterns.

The following scenarios illustrate different kinds of behaviors that directly affect test performance. Ways to deal with these problems follow the descriptions.

Scenario 1—Lacking Discipline

Joe is a nice kid, but when it comes to school and studying, he appears to lack discipline. He says things such as, "I don't have the time to study," "I'm tired," or "I'll do it later." His parents are distressed because he appears to be lazy, and they worry that he will never reach his potential.

Scenario 2—Acting Like a Smart Aleck

Sasha is viewed as aggressive and as a smart aleck. She finds reading difficult but denies that reading is challenging for her. She says she could read if she wanted to, but she just doesn't care to. Sometimes she teases classmates who are doing well in class by saying things like, "You're such a nerd. All you do is study." She often complains about her teachers and says, "They don't care about anything," or "We don't get along." Her parents realize that her behavior is interfering with her schoolwork and they worry that she'll perform poorly on the SAT.

Scenario 3—Lacking Self-Confidence

Carlos is intelligent but lacks self-confidence. He is very shy, afraid to ask questions in class, and often assumes that his teachers do not like him or care about him. Carlos is afraid of making mistakes because he feels embarrassed when he makes one and fears a bad outcome. He often cuts classes and fails to turn in homework assignments. His parents don't know how to help him improve his behavior so that he can perform to the best of his abilities.

Scenario 4—Being Overwhelmed by Anxiety

Conner is a worrier. She always thinks she will get low grades, even though she earns mostly As and Bs. She's continually checking and re-checking assignments, rewriting papers, and over-studying for exams. She has panicked on several exams and done poorly even though she knew enough to earn high marks. She displays some ineffective and self-defeating behaviors, although she is a very capable teenager. Her parents fear that her test anxiety will interfere with her doing well on the ACT.

Solving Behavior Problems

These teenagers illustrate some typical behavior problems that can interfere with effective SAT or ACT preparation. Joe lacks self-discipline and the ability to work independently. Sasha combines an academic skill problem with an inability to deal comfortably with adults, authority, or her teachers. Carlos lacks confidence in his ability, is worried about looking foolish in front of his friends, and is too shy to ask for help. Conner lacks an understanding of her strengths and how to manage her test anxiety.

All of these teenagers have developed patterns of behavior that may seem worrisome to an adult, but which help the teenagers deal with themselves, others, and the events in their daily lives. Like actors who can portray only one character, teens tend to react to all situations with the same kinds of responses, even if these responses are not particularly effective.

These students need to broaden their behaviors so that they can deal with school and people more effectively. Taking some steps to change their behaviors will, in turn, help them deal with the extra work and stress of college-admission tests. Now, let's look at some ways to resolve the problems presented in the scenarios.

Solution 1—Learning Discipline and How to Work Independently

Being able to work independently is especially important at SAT or ACT time, since preparation requires extra effort and the discipline to study. To encourage your teenager to develop the necessary self-discipline, have her answer the following questions:

- ○ What has to be done to prepare for the SAT or ACT? How should it be done?
- ○ What are the consequences of doing or not doing this preparation?

- How am I doing right now? What changes do I need to make? How do I make the changes?

After having your teen answer these questions, discuss her answers with her. Talk about how you can help her set aside time to work on her own. Helping teens learn to manage their own academic behavior involves urging them to:

- Set concrete study or test goals—for example, reading one chapter a day or taking one practice test by the end of the week

- Set their own standards and then evaluate their own study behaviors

- Design their own guidelines for how and when to study

- Decide on ways of providing themselves with incentives or rewards for sticking to a schedule

- Write their own plans for improving study behaviors

Building in rewards is an essential part of any independent work schedule. Encourage your teen to be creative in thinking of rewards. For example, you may suggest that he gets up and takes a walk around the block, has a snack, or listens to his favorite CD whenever he finishes a chunk of work.

All of these techniques are aimed at helping teenagers control themselves by becoming more aware of their own behavior. Encouraging teenagers to set their own goals does not mean that limits are no longer set by parents. It means that teenagers can be involved in the process of self-discipline. By encouraging self-discipline, you send your teenager the important message that you respect and trust him and that you see him as a valuable, skilled, and responsible individual. You give him the appropriate tools to succeed on college-admissions tests and in college, where independent study is crucial.

Solutions 2 and 3—Dealing Effectively with Authority and Teachers

Many teens find it difficult to work with adults who have authority, such as teachers and other school personnel. Some teenagers confuse cooperating with teachers, counselors, or parents with the possible loss of their personal independence. This all-or-nothing attitude makes negotiating and compromising difficult for them. Teens need to develop certain social skills in working with adults in order to achieve academic success. These skills include:

- Asking for help
- Requesting additional directions when necessary
- Answering a complaint
- Reacting to failure
- Standing up for their rights
- Being polite

Because of their inexperience, teenagers may fall into ineffective patterns of dealing with school personnel. Often, teens simply haven't yet learned how to get the skills they need. As a parent, it's a good idea to look at such problems as a lack of a skill, rather than as a flaw in character or personality. To encourage your teen to develop effective social skills, you can set aside some time to:

- Discuss the problem in terms of skills—for example, by telling him it's OK to ask for help
- Listen to and understand his concerns
- Provide new alternatives—for example, you can model how to negotiate or how to ask questions
- Arrange for practice rehearsals—have your teen rehearse how to perform new skills
- Provide verbal support

The following examples illustrate how two parents helped their teenagers improve their relationships with school personnel.

Mrs. Tino helped her daughter, Sasha, the smart aleck who had a reading problem, by first saying to her, "I know you can improve at reading. You've done well before in so many areas. I know you can learn how to do this." Then, she suggested that Sasha tell herself, "I'm good at a lot of things. It's OK to need some help." Mrs. Tino emphasized that it's not only OK to ask for help but important to do so. Then she encouraged Sasha to start a conversation with her English teacher by saying, "I understand the work, but I have a hard time reading the tests. I think I need some help."

Mr. Borges, Carlos' father, helped him learn how to ask for help by first telling him, "You're smart and you can do well in this course." He added, "Your teacher doesn't have to like you but she does have to teach you, since that's her job. I'll be here to help you, too." Then, Mr. Borges suggested that Carlos tell himself, "I do understand the material and I am going to be in class more. I need to go to class to do as well as I can in the course." Mr. Borges also encouraged Carlos to talk to this teacher and ask her, "What assignments can I make up?" Mr. Borges also helped Carlos practice approaching his teacher and saying what he needed to say. He helped Carlos set the concrete goal of making up past assignments and sticking to that goal.

Sometimes the process is painful. Teenagers deny that there is a problem, resent talking about it, blame their parents, and appear to ignore everything said. Don't be fooled though; teenagers do listen and do try out these strategies in their own time and in their own way.

Don't be discouraged if your teen appears to tune you out at first. Believe it or not, your effort means a great deal to her. Since they are in the process of learning how to act in the world, teens are flexible when it comes to changing behavior.

Solution 4—Dealing Effectively with Test Anxiety

Regardless of what they know and how well they may be doing in school, many teenagers worry about tests. Some teens' anxiety may manifest itself before, during, or after a test. Other teens may become nervous just thinking about the SAT or ACT. Still others develop anxiety when faced with difficult questions and freeze up during the test. Conner, in Scenario 4, showed typical anxiety behavior.

The following chart offers your teen guidelines for dealing with anxiety-related problems before and during the PSAT, SAT, PLAN, or ACT.

WHAT TO DO	BEFORE THE TEST	DURING THE TEST
Think positive thoughts.	"I can concentrate and study."	"I am working efficiently."
Take a positive step.	Instead of concentrating on your tension, concentrate on reading the directions for each section.	Instead of agonizing over the possibility that you won't finish in time, concentrate on working steadily and keeping calm.
Become aware of feelings.	"I am feeling tense. This is a good time to stand up and stretch."	"I am beginning to worry. This is the time to take a deep breath and try to relax."
Create positive images.	"I can see myself working efficiently."	"I remember practicing this kind of question."
Rehearse visually.	"I can see myself walk in, arrange my materials, take a deep breath, and begin to work."	"I can see myself doing this type of problem."
Breathe deeply and relax muscles.	Before beginning to study, take some deep breaths. It will help concentration.	Flex and stretch some muscles a few times each hour.
Rehearse taking the test.	Take a full-length practice test under actual exam conditions. Do it in a room at school, if possible.	Try to imagine that this is just another practice session. Having become familiar with the format and content of the test, you are as well prepared as anyone else.

OTHER RESOURCES FOR ADDRESSING BEHAVIOR

Sometimes behavior problems reach a level that results in long-term, negative effects for the teenager, such as having to repeat a grade or being suspended for long periods of time. The options open to parents seeking to break a negative chain of events include the following and are good to consider if you feel that your teen's environment is part of the problem.

○ Hire a tutor to provide support, positive learning experiences, and new strategies.

○ Change teachers, type of classes, type of curriculum, or school counselor.

○ Change schools or consider an alternative school in the same neighborhood or another regular high school in the same city.

○ Talk to an independent counselor about curriculum options, career development, or new approaches.

○ Look into a private day school or a residential boarding school.

○ Consider a fifth year of high school.

Some private schools are financially affordable, especially those that are run by religious organizations.

WORKING WITH YOUR TEEN'S GUIDANCE COUNSELOR

If you want help in dealing with behavior problems related to testing, contact your teen's teachers, school psychologist, and guidance counselor. Counselors and school psychologists are a good place to start, because they are trained to deal with student problems, have an obligation to keep confidences, and don't assign grades or administer discipline. School personnel may be able to provide one or more of the following kinds of help:

○ Information and discussion about the SAT and ACT

○ Schedules or routines to help with SAT or ACT preparation

○ Suggestions for improving self-discipline in school work

○ A support group consisting of other teenagers with similar problems

○ Incentives and/or special programs to deal with academic or behavior problems

○ Opportunities to talk to other students who have successfully dealt with similar problems

CHAPTER 8

Teenagers with Disabilities

For most teenagers, the mere thought of spending 3 hours on a Saturday morning answering SAT or ACT questions is stressful. Teenagers with disabilities feel the same pressures, but more so. This chapter discusses the special problems faced by teens with disabilities when they take college-admissions tests.

TESTING PROBLEMS EXPERIENCED BY TEENAGERS WITH DISABILITIES

Certain problems experienced by teens with disabilities when they take the SAT or ACT are obvious. For example, a blind student cannot read a regular test booklet. Many of the problems experienced by teenagers with disabilities have to do with using the test booklet and answer sheet. For instance, a teen with a learning disability may have great difficulty keeping the marks on the answer sheet in the correct order. Although time extensions are part of special testing accommodations, fatigue is still a challenge that teens with disabilities face.

Other problems are more subtle but may be equally difficult for the teenager to manage. One teen with a learning disability stated, "I hate the idea of getting accommodations for the ACT. I really don't want the other kids to know that I need more time, but I know that I need it. Also, I worry about what the college-admissions counselors will think if I use the accommodations. They say that they don't report that I use accommodations, but I worry about it anyway."

Providing your teen with correct information and handling the problems that arise empathetically will help him perform to the best of his ability in spite of the extra challenges.

BEING A SPECIAL ADVOCATE

Parents of students with disabilities are their children's most available and necessary advocates. Parents have pressured schools to provide special education services and have worked to enact legislation that mandates that all children, including those with disabilities, have the right to a free and appropriate education. Parents have fought for federal legislation to guarantee that students with disabilities who wish to go to college are able to do so. As a result of these efforts, more students with disabilities are going to college and, therefore, taking the SAT and ACT.

Teenagers with disabilities face different, and frequently more difficult, challenges when taking the SAT or ACT. If your child has a disability, you should know that special arrangements are available. In addition, you need to know how to work with school counselors, teachers, and teacher consultants so that requests for accommodations are submitted completely and in a timely manner.

Parents are required to sign their teenager's eligibility form for special accommodations.

THE PROCESS AND THE PAPERWORK

Both the SAT and ACT literature advise students and parents to discuss procedures for requesting accommodations with their high school counselors. Guidance counselors are a particularly important component of the college-admissions-test experience for students with disabilities. Counselors have all the information and forms necessary to initiate the process.

To qualify for special accommodations, students need to submit eligibility forms demonstrating their need for accommodations. After students have completed eligibility forms and obtained signatures from their parent or guardian, they must give the form to their counselor or appropriate school official. The counselor must complete the School Certification section and send the form to either the SAT's Services for Students with Disabilities office or the ACT office. Materials must arrive at the offices no later than the published deadlines. Submitting forms early ensures eligibility processing before the test date.

Your counselor's role is crucial since she has access to resources and has had experience with other students with disabilities who have taken the SAT and ACT. Your counselor can also provide guidelines for the test-preparation process.

Arranging for Special Testing Accommodations

Both the SAT and ACT administrators provide services and reasonable accommodations appropriate for various disabilities. The Americans with Disabilities Act (ADA) guarantees the right of students to have reasonable accommodations.

Standards for Accommodations

The guidelines of several professional organizations contributed to the development of the disability guidelines used by the SAT and ACT. You can access these standards at the following Web sites:

- The Association on Higher Education and Disability (AHEAD): www.ahead.org

- The Consortium on ADHD Documentation for recording attention deficit hyperactivity disorder in adolescents and adults: www.act.org/aap/disab/appx-b.html

---

Students with various disabilities and conditions are eligible to take all college-admissions tests under special testing conditions. These disabilities and conditions include:

- Blindness or vision problems

- Deafness or being hard of hearing

- Attention Deficit Hyperactivity Disorder (ADHD)

- Learning disabilities

- Certain medical conditions

- Physical disabilities

Complete information, procedures, and answers to commonly asked questions are available on the College Board and ACT Web sites:

- ☉ www.collegeboard.com/disable/students/html/indx000.html
- ☉ www.act.org/aap/disab/policy.html

You can also ask your counselor for brochures or order them from the testing services. These materials will tell you:

- ☉ Which specific disabilities are covered
- ☉ Eligibility requirements
- ☉ What documentation of an applicant's disability is needed
- ☉ The process for requesting accommodations for either the SAT or ACT
- ☉ How to submit the proper documentation in a timely manner
- ☉ The types of accommodations available

When special arrangements are required, you need to have a qualified diagnostician, such as a psychologist, neuropsychologist, or psychiatrist, provide certain information that is requested on the documents you submit. The diagnostician provides his name, title, and professional credentials. These credentials include his degrees, areas of specialization, and license or certification. The diagnostician also provides verification that the teenager has a disability that would interfere with his ability to take the test under regular testing conditions.

The fact that a student has an Individualized Educational Plan (IEP) or 504 Plan in school does not automatically guarantee that she is eligible for special testing accommodations. The student must meet eligibility requirements as defined by the SAT or ACT.

Requests for special testing must be accompanied by:

- ☉ Proof of disability provided by the diagnostician
- ☉ Proposed test date and time

⊙ Name of test administrator

⊙ The type and number of accommodations needed

If your teen does not meet all the eligibility requirements, she can request an appeal. Contact the ACT or College Board to find out how to appeal.

Keep in mind that special arrangements can be made regarding any of the following factors: time, physical arrangements, test administrator, or test materials.

Time

Some students need additional time to take the SAT or ACT. Time can be officially extended by 50 percent. When time limits are extended, additional breaks and rest periods are provided.

Physical Arrangements

Students with disabilities can request special physical arrangements (such as a table under which a wheelchair would fit) or different lighting, since fluorescent lights impact students with visual impairments. A distraction-free room is a commonly requested accommodation.

Test Administrator

The counselor or the individual requesting the arrangement for special SAT or ACT accommodations can select the test administrator. The test administrator may be the counselor or a teacher consultant. The manner in which the test administrator relates to the teenager can be critical to having the teenager feel positively about the test experience and performing to the best of her ability. The test site may be the teen's school.

Test Materials

As the standard answer sheet is unusable by many students with disabilities, large-block test booklets and answer sheets are available. The booklets are available in

Braille, large and regular type, and on cassettes. A reader, manual translator, or scribe may be used when appropriate. Sign language is also available.

The number and variety of methods used to record answers for questions is increasing as more students with disabilities take the tests. Presently, students can write or type their answers or can have someone else, called an amanuensis, write their answers. The school needs to order all of these aids at the time a request is made for special accommodations.

Working with Societal Attitudes

Society encourages the idea that effort produces success and equal opportunity is available to all. However, teenagers with disabilities are often faced with a very different message, which is: "You can't succeed no matter how hard you try." Teens with disabilities often experience the reinforcement of this message before, during, and after taking college-admissions tests.

The following remark was made by a student with cerebral palsy who used crutches but took the test under standard conditions: "The teacher (test administrator) was uncomfortable with my disability. He kept asking me questions like did I know what I was there for and did I realize the importance of the test. I felt he was questioning my mental ability."

It's important for parents and counselors of teens with disabilities to be sensitive to the teens' needs and facilitate their taking tests with minimum interference and frustration.

SPECIAL ACCOMMODATIONS AND SCORING

Beginning with the 2003–04 school year, both the SAT and ACT announced an end to the practice of *flagging*, or drawing attention to the score reports of those students who take the tests under extended-time conditions due to documented disabilities.

The decision to discontinue flagging stems from a 1999 lawsuit against the Educational Testing Service (ETS) that resulted in an agreement to remove all flags from the score reports. Parent and advocacy groups felt that flagging discouraged students from applying for needed accommodations and represented a barrier to equal access to college.

If you have advocacy-related questions, you can contact one of several organizations, including Children and Adults with ADD (CHADD), Learning Disabilities Association (LDA), and International Dyslexia Association. See the resources at the end of this chapter for more contact information.

Confidentiality is guaranteed in college-admissions testing. The protection of privacy is extended to requests, administrations, and scores of students with disabilities.

YOUR ROLE AND YOUR RIGHTS

The same basic principles that parents use to help teenagers without disabilities prepare for the SAT and ACT can be used by parents of teenagers with disabilities:

- Be informed about the SAT and ACT and how it is used
- Select a comfortable parental role
- Collect information from several sources
- Identify your teen's strengths and weaknesses
- Prepare a plan for test-taking

As a parent of a teenager with disabilities, you also need to do some additional groundwork. You need to begin thinking about college-admissions tests early, in order to prepare school personnel and locate appropriate resources, such as a tutor who understands the needs of a teen with learning disabilities as well as the test-taking requirements of the SAT or ACT.

When tutors are used, they should help teens become familiar with the kinds of special accommodations to be used during the actual test and why these accommodations are important. If an audio edition or computer will be used, the teenager should practice testing under those conditions.

The goal is to eliminate any unnecessary roadblocks that might interfere with an otherwise successful test performance. When students are familiar with a task, anxiety is reduced, precious time is saved, and undue fatigue is avoided. Prior to the actual test date, you might want to know which room will be used for the special accommodations and check on its appropriateness. Showing the room to the teenager is also a good idea.

You may also want to contact support groups and national organizations to explore your teen's rights and to get information on how to work through the usual red tape involved in getting the appropriate accommodations. Although there is awareness of the difficulties presented by the SAT and ACT to teens with disabilities, you need to be vigilant. Remember to check with medical- or mental-health professionals and school personnel that eligibility reports and applications are prepared and sent in early to the appropriate offices. You should also know that it is appropriate, and in your teenager's best interest, to directly contact college-admissions offices with questions about on-campus services and how they use SAT or ACT scores for admission purposes. Information can also be gathered from groups like Services for Students with Disabilities, which are located on most college campuses.

With the backing of federal and state legislation, the right to a college education has become more of a reality for teens with disabilities. Parents need to know that:

- ○ College-admission tests play a factor in college admissions for teens with disabilities.

- ○ Teenagers with disabilities are entitled to take the SAT or ACT regardless of negative societal attitudes.

- ○ Teenagers have the right to request appropriate accommodations that will allow them to do their best.

- ○ Scores earned by students using special accommodations are reported in the same way as those by students taking the test without accommodations.

- ○ Teenagers often need encouragement to work with their counselors, submit eligibility forms, and work with special tutors.

WORKING WITH YOUR TEEN'S GUIDANCE COUNSELOR

Many successful people remember the critical difference a good counselor made in their lives. For teens with disabilities, a knowledgeable and supportive counselor can make the difference between going or not going to college, or having a competitive or non-competitive application. Counselors can help teens in a variety of ways, including:

- ○ Helping teens see the value of taking academically challenging courses

- ○ Helping teens keep track of their progress in terms of the skills required by the SAT and ACT

- ○ Stressing the importance of analyzing the results of the PSAT or PLAN as a way of preparing for the SAT or ACT

- ○ Discussing why college-admissions tests, as well as grades, matter for college admissions and eventual college graduation

- ○ Encouraging teens who need accommodations to seek them

- ○ Explaining how to prepare eligibility forms and secure needed documentation

In addition, counselors can help you as a parent by:

- Contacting teachers to find tutors or instructional materials to improve skills in math, reading, or writing

- Discussing how to set realistic expectations and know the possibilities for positive risk-taking

- Informing you about eligibility requirements surrounding test accommodations for the SAT or ACT

- Alerting you about school or community offerings for students with disabilities—some schools host special seminars about college-admissions tests or college-application procedures that are particularly useful for students with disabilities

An early start at analyzing the results of the PSAT or PLAN helps teens, their families, and their counselors provide the information, resources, and support that is needed to take the SAT or ACT. Although teenagers with disabilities who plan to attend college and their families face special problems when preparing for college-admissions tests, there are ways to deal with these problems. The application of additional time, energy, and commitment on the part of parents, the teenager, and school personnel increase the teen's chances of succeeding on college-admissions tests.

MORE RESOURCES: ADVICE FOR TEENS WITH DISABILITIES AND THEIR PARENTS

PUBLICATIONS

Markel, G. & Greenbaum, J. *Helping Adolescents with ADHD & Learning Disabilities Ready-to-Use Tips, Techniques, and Checklists for School Success.* Hoboken, NJ: John Wiley & Sons, 2002.

Markel, G., & Greenbaum, J. *Performance Breakthroughs for Adolescents with Learning Disabilities or ADD: How to Help Students Succeed in the Regular Education Classroom.* Champaign, IL: Research Press, 1996.

Phelan, T. W. *All About Attention Deficit Disorder.* Chicago, IL: Independent Publishers Group, 2000.

Rosner, J. *Helping Children Overcome Learning Difficulties.* New York: Walker & Company, 1993.

ORGANIZATIONS AND AGENCIES

Association on Higher Education and
  Disability (AHEAD)
P.O. Box 540666
Waltham, MA 02454
Phone: 781-788-0003
Fax: 781-788-0033
E-mail: ahead@ahead.org
www.ahead.org

Children and Adults with Attention-
  Deficit/Hyperactivity Disorder
  (CHADD)
8181 Professional Place, Suite 150
Landover, MD 20785
Phone: 301-306-7070
Fax: 301-306-7090
www.chadd.org

Council for Children with Behavior
  Disorders
Council for Exceptional Children
Two Ballston Plaza
1110 North Glebe Road
Arlington, VA 22201
Phone: 800-224-6830
Fax: 703-264-9494
www.ccbd.net

Learning Disabilities Association (LDA)
4156 Library Road
Pittsburgh, PA 15234
Phone: 412-341-1515
Fax: 412 344-0224
www.ldanatl.org

National Association for Gifted
  Children (NAGC)
1707 L. Street N.W., Suite 550
Washington, D.C. 20036
Phone: 202-785-4268
E-mail: nagc@nagc.org
www.nagc.org

Recording for the Blind and Dyslexic
20 Roszel Road
Princeton, NJ 08540
Phone: 866-732-3585
www.rfbd.org

CHAPTER 9

Creating Your Plan: Preparing Your Teen for the Test

WHY CREATE A PLAN?

It takes more than good intentions to do well on a college-admissions test. It takes time, organization, and hard work. A test-prep plan provides the means for converting good intentions into meaningful test preparation. An effective plan specifies:

- ⊙ Goals
- ⊙ Responsibilities of parent and teenager
- ⊙ Available resources
- ⊙ Schedules
- ⊙ Budgets
- ⊙ Instruction
- ⊙ Possible problems or concerns

By clearly establishing who is responsible for what, a test-prep plan removes many sources of conflict between parent and teenager and allows each person to channel all of his efforts toward the goal of improving test scores. In this chapter, we'll discuss how to create a plan for your teen.

Different Problems, Different Plans

Some teenagers need to review a specific skill or subject; others have problems that require intensive instruction and practice. Since each teenager is unique, each test-prep plan must be individually tailored to fit specific needs.

A realistic short-term plan for seniors can range from two weeks to three months and may include an intensive test-taking course, a review of some specific skill, or a general review for those who are re-taking the test. On the other hand, a long-term plan can range from six months to several years.

CREATING TEST-PREP PLANS

Let's look at some step-by-step ways of creating test-prep plans and what to expect as you create a plan for your teen.

Make Time to Plan

Family life is hectic. Finding time to sit down and talk together is frequently a problem. Like a well-managed business, families with educational concerns and goals also need to have planning meetings. They need to find the time and place that will allow for discussion and working together.

Setting up a time to talk about a plan with your teen will work best if you approach her when she's most apt to be receptive. Try to avoid having the conversation when the teenager is busy or on her way out of the house. How you proceed is as important as what you do. A first step in developing a plan is to set goals.

Remember to take action in a way that is sensitive to your teen's needs and schedules.

List Goals

Goals help identify in a concrete way what you want to happen, such as your teen raising her verbal score by 40 to 60 points. Sometimes teenagers choose goals that are too general, such as doing geometry problems more accurately or completing the Critical Reading section more rapidly. Goals should be specific to the SAT or ACT even when they include study skills. For example, just having a goal of studying for 30 minutes a night does not guarantee improvement. The following list contains some sample goals.

For accuracy:	Increase the number of correct math and vocabulary test answers.
For speed:	Decrease the time needed to read comprehension exercises while maintaining an understanding of what is read.
For speed and accuracy:	Decrease the time needed to read comprehension exercises and increase understanding of what is read.
For quantity:	Increase the number of problems tried or completed.
For frequency:	Study vocabulary words and do essay writing practice exercises for about 30 minutes at least three times per week.
For duration:	Increase study sessions to 1 hour, adding additional practice math problems.

After outlining the goals, the next step in planning is to prepare a schedule.

Make a Schedule

A test-preparation schedule should include a timetable and weekly or daily activity lists. First make the timetable. You can use a regular calendar that covers the time between the current date and the date of the SAT or ACT. To make your timetable, write down all activities related to preparing for the test and the test date on the calendar. The following example illustrates the benefit of creating a timetable.

Jane, a junior, was worried about her SAT scores. She scored about 400 on the Critical Reading section and 435 on the Math section on practice exams. Jane lives in a rural community and needs to schedule some of her SAT studying during the summer when special programs are offered in a nearby city. Her timetable extended over an 18-month period and included several different activities, including the shaded region marking her field hockey practice. One activity was to use a commercially available SAT book to practice test-taking within specific time limits. Another was to review geometry. Although she had planned to visit relatives in the summer, after she had filled in her timetable, she saw that she would have to shorten her travel plans in order to take a commercial SAT course in August. Her schedule follows.

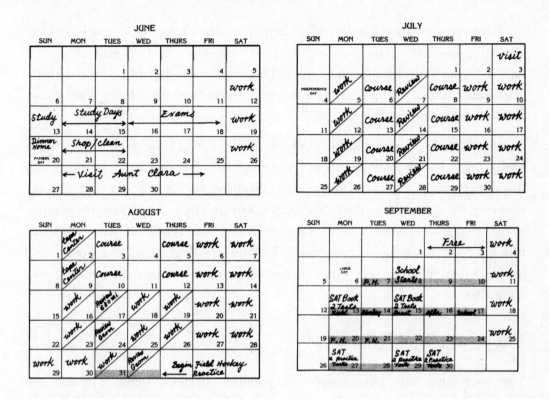

You should also keep weekly and/or daily lists to identify specific tasks, such as the type or number of practice exercises to be completed. Such scheduling spells out the tasks ahead of time, reduces unnecessary worrying, and allows for more realistic planning. Often, teenagers become overwhelmed by the thought of all that has to be done and end up doing nothing. Writing a list and assigning times to each task tends to make these jobs more doable and more realistic.

Talk about Costs

Although you want to do everything possible for your teen's college-admissions test preparation, cost is an important consideration. Most families' budgets are already strained without adding the expenses of materials, tutors, or commercial courses—especially since test preparation comes at a time when parents are trying to save up money for college tuition.

Regardless of who pays the bill—the parent, the teenager, or both—budgets should be discussed. The estimated costs of various alternatives should also be outlined. Any budget limits and expected responsibilities should be proposed. By discussing these issues up front, you clarify problems and provide a realistic basis for decision-making.

Consider the case of Delores. Delores knew that her family was on a tight budget. She hesitated talking about a tutor because she knew her Dad didn't like discussing money, neither did he like saying no to something related to schoolwork. However, she did bring up the subject and discovered that a small amount of money was available—enough to allow her and several friends to share the expenses of hiring a tutor. If she had not discussed the budget with her Dad, she would have assumed that no money was available and she might have missed out on tutoring altogether.

Find Out about Resources

Your community may have a variety of resources to help teenagers prepare for college-admissions tests. However, it may take a little detective work to find them. For example, many religious groups sponsor young-adult activities. These groups usually know skilled people within the community who would be willing to help teenagers study for the SAT or ACT. In addition, parent or community groups may also be willing to sponsor special activities if they are aware of teenagers' needs.

Match Materials to Your Teen's Goals

You and your teen should now select which books, equipment, and/or specialized materials will be used. You should match these materials with your teenager's goals. Consider drawing on information from teachers or counselors, previous standardized tests, and test-prep books that analyze the PSAT, PLAN, SAT, or ACT. Material can be purchased, borrowed, or shared by several teenagers. See the "List of Resources" for test-related materials.

Locate a Tutor

In finding a tutor, you should consider someone who has experience with the college-admissions tests. You may actually hire more than one tutor, since instruction may be provided by volunteers, peers, schoolteachers, or professional tutors. Discuss various tutoring options with your teen.

Keep in mind that expertise is needed not only with the subject area but also with the SAT or ACT format and with effective test-taking techniques.

Find a Place to Practice and Study

Regardless of your plan's specifics, your teen needs a suitable place in which to study. Teenagers who register for courses or who receive tutoring have to practice test-taking at home too. It is important to select a quiet study place at home or at school for SAT or ACT homework assignments or for sessions with the tutor. It is also smart to turn off phones, the TV, and computers to reduce interruptions and distractions while your teen is preparing for the test.

A place to study doesn't have to be a separate room. Some teens work well as long as they have a desk and a quiet, well-lit space.

Expect the Unexpected

Not surprisingly, there are always some unanticipated problems or unexpected events that crop up during the test-prep process. Teenagers and tutors get sick, courses may be wrong for the teenager, personality conflicts may develop, and people may forget to do what they said they'd do.

While everyone is calm and optimistic, it's helpful to discuss potential problems and possible resolutions. Consider our example.

Rainer was a senior and had a pattern of talking big and making promises. His parents were concerned because they felt he would not follow through and take an ACT course, no matter how much they talked and planned. However, they did not want to force the issue by insisting that he go. Besides, they weren't willing to pay unless Rainer agreed that he needed to go. When the family discussed a possible plan, Rainer said he wanted to study on his own, using his brother's books. The parents suggested that if, by chance, he did not follow the independent study plan, he would then register for the commercial course and pay at least some of the fee himself. Rainer agreed. His parents felt that they had been responsible and had provided ways for Rainer to exercise his independence. They anticipated a possible problem and agreed with their teen upon a way to deal with things, if the problem occurred.

For some parents, brief meetings to discuss potential problems are already a part of family life. Each family needs to find its own methods. The important part is to anticipate issues and discuss ways in which they can be handled.

WORKING WITH YOUR TEEN'S GUIDANCE COUNSELOR

Counselors can assist teens in developing a reasonable timetable, one that permits regular schoolwork, with SAT or ACT preparation integrated into it. The counselor can help teens break down the larger assignments, such as reviewing vocabulary, into more digestible chunks. For example, the counselor can guide teens to work on 20 new words a week, learning 5 words per day and using one day for review. A long-range plan might be to try to raise a verbal score by 50 to 75 points. A short-term plan might include regularly working on those areas that were not particularly strong on previous tests.

CREATING *YOUR* TEST-PREP PLAN

Now that you have a good idea of what creating a test-prep plan involves, you can begin creating your plan, tailored to the needs of your teen.

Set the Stage

Sometimes it seems that the best family discussions take place in the car, where there is no easy exit and distractions are few. Regardless of where your planning discussion occurs, you should reduce distracting factors and write down mutually agreed upon decisions. Before sitting down with your teen to start planning, be ready in the following ways:

- Be prepared to do a "subtle sell job"
- Avoid dwelling on past mistakes or failures
- Review the information you've gathered
- Ask questions, and then be ready to listen
- Don't threaten by saying things like, "You'll never get into college unless you study for the SAT!"
- Assume that your teenager means well, but may not be aware of the long-term consequences of being unprepared for the test

Discuss the Costs and Benefits of Test Preparation

At the start of your planning process, you should discuss the costs and benefits of the potential test-prep plan. Remember that parents and teens may have very different perspectives on costs and benefits.

In terms of the college-admissions test, the long-term benefit to you is knowing that you have helped your teenager realize that hard work pays off and that the SAT or ACT is the first step toward the larger goal of college and career. Test preparation offers you an opportunity to help your teenager assume responsibility, work toward a long-term goal, and make important decisions. You need to keep in mind that while some negative short-term costs, such as money, time, or arguments, will be incurred, the long-term benefits far outweigh the costs.

When you initiate a discussion about costs and benefits with your teen, keep in mind the following points:

⊙ Be supportive of your teen's college or career goals

⊙ Ask questions based on information you've collected about the tests

⊙ Raise important issues, but leave final decisions for consideration by your teen

⊙ Avoid ridiculing, undermining, or criticizing your teen by saying things such as, "You're not even studying for the SAT!"

During these discussions, help your teenager look toward the future and define long-term costs and benefits.

Specifically, you may want to discuss the following probable expenses of SAT or ACT prep:

Time: To talk, listen, gather information, drive, or organize schedules. Time is an especially important factor when families are large, single parents are in charge, or both parents work.

Money: To pay for books, the test fee, tutors, or transportation. Money is always an important factor, but it becomes especially critical when parents are saving for college.

Energy: To assume more responsibility, more patience, or more concern.

A Teenager's View of the Costs and Benefits

Teenagers are concerned with the present. They are more in tune with daily happenings, like basketball games or dates, than with plans for the future. This short-term outlook makes the parent's job more difficult in helping the teen prepare for the SAT or ACT. When teenagers consider test preparation, their immediate reaction is to accentuate the negative costs, such as the extra time, extra energy, or possible risks, and to ignore the long-term positive gains, such as scholarships, increased choices, and feelings of achievement. As a parent, you should be prepared to remind your teen of what's at stake.

Using Materials Efficiently and Effectively

Once materials are selected and made available, you need to be sure they are used efficiently and effectively. Learning occurs more rapidly and is better retained when:

- ⚬ Information is meaningful
- ⚬ Attention is focused on a task
- ⚬ Skills are used and required in situations other than testing
- ⚬ Skills are practiced in a testing situation and under simulated testing conditions

Do a Subtle Sell Job

Doing a subtle sell job means helping your teenager realize that the long-term benefits of test preparation outweigh the short-term costs of studying. As you prepare to make a test-prep plan with your teen, you may want to use the following chart to guide your thinking about the plan's importance.

		COSTS (TIME, MONEY, ENERGY)	BENEFITS (SUPPORT, CHALLENGE, ACHIEVEMENT)
PARENTS	**SHORT-TERM**	"It takes me 20 minutes to drive to the tutor."	"I know I helped."
		"I've already spent $20 on books."	"Her scores went up."
		"I'm tired of thinking and talking about the SAT.	"I feel good."
		"I wasn't liked when I suggested an SAT course."	"He knows we care."
	LONG-TERM	"I ought to have spent more time."	"He did the best he could."
		"It's costing twice as much now."	"She got into three colleges."
		"I should have been firmer about SAT studying."	"Now I can relax."
		"I wish I had been more aware."	"She knows we all worked to help her."
TEENAGERS	**SHORT-TERM**	"I'd rather be sleeping."	"Studying takes time, but it's OK."
		"The SAT fee is so high!"	"I stopped worrying when I started studying."
		"I'm tired of studying."	"I'm learning how to take tests."
		"I don't feel like caring."	"My math is actually improving."
		"Suppose I don't do well?"	"I'm learning new words."
		"No one else is studying."	"This is a first step toward being a lawyer."
	LONG-TERM	"I didn't get into the college I wanted. I hope I can transfer later."	"My scores were high and I won a scholarship."
		"I could have done better."	"I did the best I could."
		"I should have listened to my parents."	"I had a good choice of colleges."
		"I wish I had tried harder."	"My parents helped a lot."

Being subtle means discussing such issues in ways that allow your teenager to accept help without too much resentment and defensiveness. This is not an easy job, but it is certainly worth the effort. The following example shows how a well-meaning parent misses this essential point.

Franklin and his dad are discussing SAT preparation. Mr. Beaumont is an efficient executive and recognizes that time schedules and time management are important parts of long-term planning. He assumes that his son will follow his example. Mr. Beaumont was surprised, angry, and disappointed when he learned that his son had done nothing to prepare for the SAT. He really wants to help his son, but he made the following comments during their conversation:

"Listen to me. I know what to do. I've been doing time management for years."

"No one ever taught me to do this. When I was your age I had to learn everything myself."

"If you weren't fooling around so much, you probably wouldn't need me to show you any of this."

"Did you write a schedule yet? You said you would."

"I knew you wouldn't be able to organize yourself!"

The ending to this discussion is predictable: Franklin walks out of the room and Mr. Beaumont stalks into the living room and says to his wife, "I don't know what's going on with your son. I keep trying to help him, but I don't get anywhere."

This parent forgot that it took him a long time to acquire his skills and that the best way to help his son learn time-management skills is to design a situation in which his son can learn those skills independently. He also bullied, criticized, and nagged his son.

Mr. Beaumont might have had greater success with Franklin had he adopted one of the following strategies:

- **Asking a question,** such as, "Would you like me to help you write a schedule?"

- **Providing an example** by saying something such as, "Sounds like you have to organize your time. I do too. Would you like to see how I set up my schedule?"

- **Sharing feelings in a positive manner** by saying something like, "I'm a little surprised you haven't begun to study. Is there a problem?"

- **Acknowledging the costs and accentuating the benefits** by saying something like, "I know it's a pain, but studying will help you get what you want."

Remember that how you go about creating your teen's test-prep plan is as important as the actual details of the plan.

It's never too early to start planning for college-admissions tests. Even if your teen is only in her sophomore year, you should map out what lies ahead. Planning ahead ensures that important concerns are provided for and allows for choices as decisions are made later.

Discuss Goals

After your discussion of the costs and benefits of test preparation, discuss some goals with your teen. Goals should be challenging, positive, and realistic in terms of the teenager's strengths and weaknesses. Teens need a lot of positive support. Try to encourage your teenager by frequently making supportive comments and keep in mind that:

- Your teenager is in a period of change and adults can't always predict what his later achievement will be. Therefore, you should accent the positive whenever possible and try to set high, but realistic, goals.

- Your teenager is in a period of development when his self-confidence and feelings about himself are based on what he thinks others think about him. Being supportive and having high expectations of him will enable him to find ways to meet those expectations.

- Teenagers often base their opinions of themselves on their friends' views of them. Often these views have to do with looks, personality, or athletic ability and not with academic or intellectual achievement. Although they are good students, teenagers who are poor athletes may feel totally inadequate.

⊙ Some of the information that teenagers use in evaluating themselves, especially when it is based on their friends' views, may be irrelevant, inaccurate, or incomplete. Such information is not useful in terms of positively influencing teenagers' ideas of themselves or how they should prepare for the SAT or ACT.

It might be reasonable for some teens to aim for an increase of 50–100 points on each section of a test. However, setting a goal that includes a more realistic range of points, such as 30 to 50 points, reduces the risk of disappointment and increases the possibility and pleasant experience of earning even higher scores.

Bear in mind, too, that teenagers tend to think in terms of "all or nothing." Either they think they can do anything and everything on the SAT or ACT, or they think they can't improve at all and that the test doesn't count. It's the adult's responsibility to provide clear guidelines and to help with the planning process. Realistic goals tend to set the stage for success.

Set Schedules

Some teens work in a slow and plodding manner, while others start off with great gusto and then develop a more moderate, but constant, pace. The best pattern is the one that works. Therefore, your teenager may have to experiment with different schedules to find the one that is most productive. Use these guidelines to help you and your teenager establish an effective test-prep plan.

⊙ Set up several short study periods over a long period of time.

⊙ Vary the nature of study sessions. For example, one night your teenager can study with a friend, another night she can work with you, and once every two weeks she can work with a group of students.

⊙ Reschedule chores so that they don't interfere with study time.

⊙ Be realistic about schedules.

There are numerous ways to change your teen's chores to create a better study schedule during SAT or ACT prep. For example, your teenager is responsible for cleaning the dinner dishes. Instead, you might want to change the chores so that your teenager has some early-morning responsibilities, such as making lunches, which do not interfere with studying after dinner.

Teenagers are usually aware of how long they can study effectively. Starting with her usual attention span, your teen can begin to increase her study time, perhaps from 20 to 30 minutes to 50 minutes per session. Using a daily or weekly time schedule, have your teen fill in all the things she must do and identify the times during which she is most likely to be able to study and concentrate. Her chores, dates, extracurricular activities, and jobs can then be worked around the test schedule. Sometimes, jobs and extracurricular activities have to be the first items that are written down and the SAT or ACT study sessions have to be worked around those activities.

To set up a workable schedule, use a one-year or eighteen-month calendar to plan the following types of events:

○ Dates on which the tests are administered

○ School or family vacations

○ Job obligations

○ Major extracurricular events

After doing that, use a two- to six-month calendar to schedule test-preparation activities between the first proposed test date and the present. Once you've mapped out the big picture, begin using weekly or daily agendas to remind you of the specific tasks that need to be accomplished.

Remember to select a comfortable role in SAT or ACT preparation. Your responsibilities may include projecting a budget, locating tutors, contacting organizations, or purchasing materials, among other tasks. The important thing is to systematically approach these tasks in order to help your teen achieve his goals.

Write Your Plan

As you create your plan and revise it, you and your teen should list specific responsibilities, as well as the expected and actual costs. Use the following outline to help you keep notes.

Describe the planning time:
Identify goals:
Set schedules and agendas:
List possible materials, instructors, and/or locations:
Identify resources:
Assign responsibilities and roles:
Specify costs and budgets:

Review and Revise Your Plan

After writing an initial plan, you should review it to make sure it's realistic. Remember that you can and should revise your plan as you go along. The following questions will help you and your teenager determine whether your plan is relevant, realistic, and useful.

PLANNING TIME

☐ Has a specific time been selected?

☐ Has a quiet, comfortable place been chosen?

☐ Has all the necessary information been collected?

☐ Have costs and benefits been discussed?

☐ Have roles for both the parent and teenager been discussed?

GOALS

☐ Have the teen's strengths been discussed?

☐ Have problems been identified and prioritized according to time and/or financial constraints?

☐ Have goals been discussed and written?

☐ Are the goals realistic?

☐ Are the goals listed in the order of their importance?

☐ Has a range of outcomes been considered (such as increasing scores by 25 to 50 points on the ACT science section)?

SCHEDULE

☐ Has a timetable that specifies all time commitments been designed?

☐ Does the schedule seem realistic in terms of goals and limitations?

☐ Have tutoring sessions been scheduled?

☐ Have study or practice sessions been scheduled?

☐ Have time limits been specified for those sessions?

MATERIALS

☐ What materials are needed?

☐ How are materials matched with goals or problems?

☐ How will materials be used?

☐ Who is responsible for acquiring the materials?

COACHES AND INSTRUCTORS

☐ Who will provide the coaching or instruction?

☐ Does this person have the necessary skills?

☐ Are other teachers or tutors necessary?

LOCATION

☐ Where will instruction occur?

☐ Has transportation been arranged?

☐ When studying at home, where will it be done?

☐ Will these places be available when needed?

BUDGET

☐ Have financial costs and resources been discussed?

☐ Have financial responsibilities been specified?

☐ If costs are a problem, have alternatives been considered and discussed?

☐ Are adjustments or alternatives necessary?

RESOURCES

☐ Have the necessary or desired resources been identified?

☐ Who is responsible for selecting and contacting these resources?

☐ How will decisions be made about the usefulness of these resources?

WORKING WITH YOUR TEEN'S GUIDANCE COUNSELOR

Counselors have a great deal of experience in designing course schedules. In writing a test-prep plan, one of the components is a realistic schedule. Teens work differently; some are slow while others race through the work. Counselors can help customize schedules to meet the needs of individual teens.

You should consider the plan to be an experiment and adjust as your particular situation changes. In the next chapter, we'll discuss how to manage your plan once it's initiated.

CHAPTER 10
Managing Your Plan

Have you ever found yourself staring blankly at supermarket shelves because your carefully prepared shopping list was left on the kitchen table? Although you took time to plan, the plan was useless, since you didn't have it in hand to follow. In order to make sure that goals are reached after creating your test-prep plan, you need to manage the plan. This means checking on progress, fixing problems, and making necessary changes.

ANTICIPATE POSSIBLE HURDLES

Some common problems that arise during the test-prep process include:

- The teenager hates the tutor.
- The instructor gets sick.
- The study group falls apart due to conflict.
- One of the parents loses a job, so money is no longer available for a commercial course.

More subtle problems can occur when:

- Teenagers set unrealistic goals and then feel tired, frustrated, and angry.
- Parents become worried that their teenager isn't making enough progress.
- Parents feel angry and disappointed when things don't work out exactly as planned.

When managing a plan, you must assume that problems will arise and that plans have to be changed to deal with these problems. Helping your teenager shift gears and learn how to make adjustments is vital preparation for the real world and a valuable skill for her to learn now.

STAYING ON TRACK

Your teenager needs to know how she is doing while preparing for the test, so that she can, if necessary, change plans. To illustrate this point, consider the case of Wendy.

Wendy had an SAT test-prep plan and had been following it for about two weeks. Her goal was to increase her critical reading scores, especially by learning more vocabulary. She had planned to learn about 30 new words twice a week. When she told her father that she didn't feel like she was getting anywhere, he replied, "Oh, Wendy, don't worry. You're probably doing fine. Just keep up the good work."

Wendy's father's comments were kind, but both Wendy and her father needed specific information on her performance in order to decide whether or not the plan needed to be changed.

Ways to Track Progress

Here are some ways you can check on your teen's performance progress:

- Keep records for each study session
- Keep track of the number of problems completed correctly
- Keep track of how much time it takes to complete the work
- Review the records to see if changes to the plan need to be made
- Make sure your teen is focused on the specific SAT or ACT sections or questions that need special attention

Teenagers can check on their progress in several ways. These methods include calendars, checklists, charts, and graphs. The best method is the one that your teen will regularly use.

Research suggests that knowing how you are doing can positively influence your performance. Remember the days when you put your children's drawings on the refrigerator? Recognition still goes a long way. Post progress charts where they can be seen and praised.

Calendars

Calendars provide an easy and handy way of keeping track of progress. When using a calendar, have your teenager first circle the dates set aside for SAT or ACT studying. Then, she can fill in the circle for those days when studying actually occurred. Wendy had circled Tuesdays and Thursdays for vocabulary practice. She planned to study and did study on the 2nd , 4th, and 9th. Although she planned to study on the 11th, 16th, and 18th, she did not follow through because she was sick. Her monthly calendar looked like this:

Wendy's Calendar

S	M	T	W	T	F	S
	1	②	3	④	5	6
7	8	⑨	10	⑪	12	13
14	15	⑯	17	⑱	19	20

Circled = Planned   Shaded = Completed

Checklists

Checklists can be used to keep track of chores and activities or to list procedures that need to be followed. For example, Steve really fell apart when he took tests that were timed. He could feel himself getting tense even when he did timed practice tests at home. With the help of his guidance counselor, Steve wrote a list of steps to follow when he was taking timed math practice tests. After taking each practice test, he put an X next to the steps he had completed. Some days he followed all of the steps and on other days he did not. His checklist for four sessions looked like this:

Steve's Checklist

Steps	Sessions			
	1	2	3	4
1. Count the number of questions to see how much time is available per problem.	x		x	x
2. Quickly skim over all the questions.	x	x		x
3. First do the easiest questions.		x	x	x
4. Guess on familiar questions.		x	x	x
5. Check for careless errors.	x			x

Charts

Since her main problem was the math section on the ACT, Naima kept a daily list of the time she spent on each type of question. She had planned to spend 1 hour, three times a week, doing different types of math exercises. She used an ACT practice book and made a simple daily chart. Her chart for a week looked like this:

Naima's Chart

MONDAY	WEDNESDAY	FRIDAY
1. Roots and radicals	1. Verbal problems	1. Inequalities
2. Do 30 problems	2. Algebra problems	2. Do 20 problems
3. Check answers	3. Do 20 problems	3. Check answers
4. Review mistakes	4. Check answers	4. Review mistakes

Graphs

Graphs can provide a visual picture of your teenager's progress. He can keep track of the number of words learned, the percentage of questions answered correctly, or the number of questions completed within a certain time period.

Mark needed to improve his critical reading skills. His goal was to keep up his understanding of what he read while trying to read faster. His teacher helped him make a graph to plot his rate (the number of words divided by the number of minutes) and his accuracy (the percentage of questions correctly answered). Mark's graph showed him that he was improving his speed, and although at first, the number of questions correctly answered dropped, he soon returned to his original critical reading score of 80 percent.

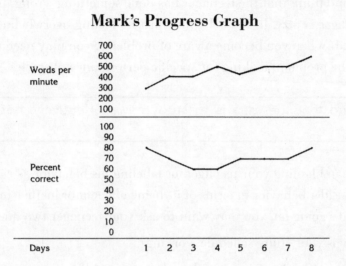

Mark's Progress Graph

Timing Your Comments

You should comment on performance when the progress has occurred, not a week or two later. Teenagers usually do not want anyone to know that they are studying for the tests, so it's best to comment when no one else is around. You should also be especially sensitive to how your teenager will receive any comments about her work. Teenagers often view these helpful hints as criticism, even when they are offered in a positive way. You may find it easier to use notes or humor as a way of making a point that can be accepted by your teen. For example, Anne's mother wrote her the following note:

> *Dear Anne:*
>
> *I see that you're keeping track of the number of problems you com-*
> *plete for the SAT. Looks like you're doing at least 2–3 more problems*
> *each time—HOORAY!*

FIXING PROBLEMS

When teenagers are not progressing as anticipated, parents frequently jump to conclusions and think that the teenager has done something wrong. It may appear that the teenager is lazy. In fact, she may just be feeling overwhelmed, confused, and exhausted. When you become aware of problems, you may need to take a second look at the problem, looking for specific performance obstacles.

Keep in mind that the idea is to study more effectively, not necessarily longer.

Rather than blaming your teenager, or labeling his behavior as right or wrong, you might consider behavior in terms of its being efficient or inefficient. To help you pinpoint what's going on, you may want to ask your teenager two questions:

- How is your study schedule working?
- Are you learning what you thought you would?

Your teen can give you the information to zero in on the specific problem. Some common problems teenagers face concern unrealistic goals, unsuitable materials, and inefficient organization.

Applying Solutions

Usually there is more than one solution for every identified problem. Here are some common SAT and ACT test-prep problems and a variety of possible solutions.

Problem: The teen seems to give up because it appears to him that the material is too complicated.

Solution: Divide the assignments into smaller parts or find a different tutor.

Problem: Progress is slower than anticipated and not enough time is left to reach the original goal.

Solutions: Lower the expectations about the scores.

Rearrange the study schedule.

Provide more intensive instruction.

Take the test date at a later date.

Shoot for a later college-admissions date.

Problem: The teenager is studying, but does not remember anything the next day.

Solutions: Change from group to individual tutoring.

Change from reading the information to listening to some of the information.

Practice aloud before doing the test exercises.

Study in a different place.

Check that the teaching materials are matched to the skills needed.

Problem: The teenager is studying, but seems to lose things and waste time.

Solution: Give her information and techniques that will help her to become better organized.

Problem: The teenager seems frantic and appears to be spending too much time studying.

Solution: Provide some written material that will help him rank what has to be done in order of importance.

Review the goals, costs, and benefits, but keep in mind that the test is part of a larger picture.

Using Checklists to Manage Problems

It is important that teenagers try to manage their own problems. However, sometimes they lack the information they need to effectively deal with these problems. Use the following checklists to help your teenager learn how to manage her own problems.

ORGANIZING MATERIALS

DO YOU:

☐ Have papers and books that you haven't looked at for months?

☐ Waste time and break up your concentration looking for things you have misplaced?

☐ Lose test registration papers, exercise sheets, or materials?

☐ Have a study area that is a mess?

☐ Let things pile up because you don't know where to put them?

THEN TRY TO:

☐ Schedule periodic clean-ups. Throw out the things you don't use.

☐ Find the necessary papers and materials before starting to study.

☐ Arrange your materials in a systematic manner, such as by using folders.

☐ Make a labeled file or box for different kinds of materials.

☐ Store your materials and supplies in an easy-to-spot place.

ORGANIZING TIME

DO YOU:

☐ Let assignments pile up because you can't decide what to do first?

☐ Forget regular school assignments that you can't study for as you had planned?

☐ Have a hard time sticking to your study schedule?

☐ Forget to do errands, like picking up materials or making phone calls?

☐ Find that your attention wanders when you begin to study?

THEN TRY TO:

☐ Write down all your assignments—by the week or by the day—putting those that should be done first at the top of the list.

☐ Ask teachers for all future test or project dates and write them down on your calendar.

☐ See how long you can study and regularly increase this time in 5- to 10-minute intervals.

☐ Write yourself notes and put them on your backpack or wallet. This looks funny but it works.

☐ Ask yourself, "At what time do I study best?" Change your study time if necessary.

ORGANIZING TASKS

DO YOU:

☐ Try to cram everything in?

☐ Feel anxious if you don't have every minute planned?

☐ Feel uncomfortable if you need to change your schedule?

☐ Feel overburdened by the responsibilities of test preparation?

☐ Want to study but don't, because someone asks you to do something else?

☐ Find the work difficult?

THEN TRY TO:

☐ Be selective. Do only those tasks that are the most important.

☐ Make sure that you allow time to relax and exercise.

☐ Tell yourself, "Relax and be flexible. I have a schedule and I'll do the best I can."

☐ Get a study buddy you can call when you get discouraged.

☐ Practice saying, "No. I'd really like to but I'm studying."

☐ Give yourself a pep talk and say, "This is hard, but it can be done."

MOTIVATING YOUR TEENAGER

Once you get the plan going, the next step is to keep it going. Studying for the test usually isn't fun. It is hard work and teenagers need encouragement to keep going.

Sometimes teenagers are motivated because they can immediately taste success. For example, Rico studied for a chemistry test and received an A. It is highly likely that he will study for the next test because he saw that his work paid off.

Checking on progress on the SAT or the ACT practice tests is important. Doing so gives your teenager the opportunity to realize that her work does pay off and progress is being made.

Sometimes parents need to boost motivation when they see signs of fatigue or signals that their teenager is being turned off to studying. If you are trying to find ways to encourage your teenager, consider the following:

- Make positive statements, such as "I know you're working hard"

- Provide extra treats, such as a special dinner or extra use of the car

- Leave a small, silly gift, such as a huge pencil, key ring, etc.

- Organize some special event, such as going to the movies, a concert, out to eat, or to dinner with another family whose teenager is also taking the test

- Do some chore for your teenager so that your teen can study

Setting Up Rewards

Sometimes, you need to put into practice methodical and consistent ways to make sure that plans are followed. In other words, you may need to make sure that certain events occur after, and only after, a task is completed. The following examples show how you can build in rewards for work that was accomplished.

Ron tends to be forgetful. For a month, he had not done the vocabulary exercises he agreed to do. He and his parents worked out a plan so that if a certain number of exercises were completed on Tuesday and Thursday nights, he could have the car on Fridays.

Diana, on the other hand, did not want the car—she loved talking on the phone. Her family devised a plan that required her to work on her writing exercises for 30 minutes, three nights a week, before she could talk on the phone.

Regardless of the system of rewards, remember to be positive, low-key, and avoid negative or punishing situations. The goal is to encourage and support effective studying, not to control your teenager. By establishing realistic goals and rewards, you help your teenager do her best and show her that you really care.

This final list of questions is provided to help you check on your teen's progress and iron out problems. When plans are well-managed, trouble spots are easily identified and changes can usually be made without anyone feeling that he has failed, especially the teenager.

☐ Is progress being checked using charts, checklists, graphs, or other means?

☐ Do charts or graphs show any problems?

☐ What adjustments are necessary?

☐ Have alternative solutions been considered?

☐ Are any additional resources or checklists necessary?

☐ Has progress been made toward the goals?

WORKING WITH YOUR TEEN'S GUIDANCE COUNSELOR

Counselors can help by scheduling appointments with your teen to discuss how he is managing his test-prep plans. Your teen's guidance counselor can also offer suggestions about ways to modify the plan or improve study strategies if things are not working well. For example, she may suggest meeting with a particular teacher for additional instruction or review, a summer school opportunity, or a special tutor. As with other steps in the test-prep process, working with your teen's guidance counselor can save lots of time, energy, and frustration for everyone.

CHAPTER 11
Beyond the SAT and ACT

Your teen might think that her work ends the day the SAT or ACT is taken. However, after he takes the test, he should engage in several follow-up activities. These activities include:

- Requesting his test booklet and answer sheet from the test publisher. This request may be made up to 120 days after his scores have been released.

- Checking his answers against the correct answers to make certain no scoring errors were made. Students can and should ask to have the test rescored if they believe that there has been an error in scoring.

You might ask, "Why bother to check your answers?" and "What difference can one or two errors make?" The answers are that errors are made and that discovering these errors can have far-reaching effects. Consider what happened when students who took the PSAT and SAT reported errors:

What Happened? A Florida student reported an error on the PSAT. The Educational Testing Service (ETS) acknowledged that the student's answer was correct.

The Effects:

- Approximately 240,000 students' PSAT scores increased.

- An estimated 200 additional students qualified as semifinalists for National Merit Scholarships.

- Before the error was discovered, approximately 80,000 students who previously took an SAT in which this question was included were incorrectly penalized.

What Happened? A high school student in New York reported an error on the SAT after he received his copy of his test and answers. The error was confirmed by ETS.

The Effects:

- Approximately 16,000 students' SAT scores increased.

- Approximately 250 of those students then qualified for state scholar-ships.

Students have a right to this information under the Truth-in-Testing Law, which has been passed in several states. Currently, all students, nationally, can receive their SAT answers and the answer sheet. In order to receive this "test package," the student is responsible for making the request to ETS and for enclosing a check to cover the costs.

WHAT TO DO AFTER RECEIVING TEST MATERIALS

Once test scores and booklets have been received, the materials should be carefully reviewed using the following questions.

GENERAL SCORES

- Is there a significant difference between the verbal and mathematical portions?

- Is there a pattern of incorrect answers (e.g., the scores are lower as the test progresses)?

- Does the answer sheet look as though some single error was made that accounts for a high number of errors (e.g., the wrong box was filled in and then all the rest of the answers were incorrectly marked)?

- Do the scores show the expected levels of achievement?

- Were there any problems that interfered with the students' performance (e.g., ran out of time)?

SUBTEST SCORES

○ Do the subtests indicate any specific skill weakness?

○ Are scores on the subtests in keeping with the expected results (e.g., student has a B+ average in English, but is weak on SAT comprehension questions)?

ITEM ANALYSIS

○ What types of errors occurred (e.g., difficulty with word problems)?

○ Where do errors occur most frequently (e.g., beginning, middle, end)?

○ Are questions frequently not answered?

○ Where are the questions frequently not answered (e.g., beginning, middle, end)?

○ Does it seem that time was a problem (e.g., all answered questions are answered accurately, but the subtest is not completed)?

HAVE YOUR TEEN REFER TO THESE QUESTIONS AFTER TAKING THE TEST.

☐ Have answers and the answer key been requested?

☐ Who will review and analyze the test?

☐ When will this review occur?

☐ Are results positive enough?

☐ Is a retake necessary?

☐ When will the retake occur?

THEN DECIDE:

☐ Should the SAT or ACT be taken again?

☐ When will the next test be given?

☐ What plans must be made?

☐ Should a test-prep course be taken?

RETAKING THE TEST

If you are or your teen is dissatisfied with his test score, he can take the test again by registering for a future test date. A new test, with entirely different questions, is administered each time the test is repeated. Some colleges look at the highest SAT score taken if more than one test score is reported; others average the scores. Students who repeat the test usually do better on the second or third round.

A National Educational Association study found that a group of students who were coached between their first and second SAT improved by an average of 104 points. The average increase of those who were not coached, but repeated the test, was 44 points. Repeating the test without studying will probably not make a large difference in SAT or ACT scores. If your teen wants to retake the test, with or without coaching, you need to again implement a test-prep plan, just as you did the first time around.

WORKING WITH YOUR TEEN'S SCHOOL

Even during recent times when the national SAT and ACT scores have declined, the average scores for some schools have increased or stayed the same. Your teen's school plays a large part in how well prepared she will be to take college-admissions tests. As a parent, you can help shape how effective your teen's school is when it comes to test preparation. Here are some things you can do to influence your teenager's school's test-prep programs:

- Call the guidance office to discuss SAT or ACT test-prep-related concerns with your teen's counselor.

- Join an already existing parent-teacher organization.

- Get together with other families and alternate attending various meetings that influence school policy.

- Ask the principal to become more involved with the curriculum as it relates to the SAT or ACT.

- Understand what you want as a parent and how you can support school personnel as they help your teenager prepare for college-admissions tests.

You can also ask the guidance office to provide services related to the tests such as:

○ Group or individual counseling sessions providing descriptions of college prerequisites and preadmission tests

○ Encouraging teenagers to enroll in more academic courses

○ Providing sessions to analyze the PLAN, ACT, PSAT, and SAT

Advocating for Your Teen

Remember that an advocate speaks for an individual's welfare by recognizing needs and inadequacies in services and identifying needed resources. An advocate attempts to create a workable match between needs and resources.

Regardless of your roles during the test-prep process, being involved and making school personnel aware of your interest and concerns can create positive results for your teen. Here are some more suggestions for working with your teen's school:

○ Encourage the school to provide continuous progress reports on the quantity and quality of your teenager's academic work.

○ Support the use of essay-type test questions in subjects other than English.

○ Demand the recognition and status for academic achievement that exists for sports, such as honors ceremonies or banquets.

○ Suggest a resource room or special space in the library where students may practice independently, using self-instructional books.

○ Compliment and support those teachers and staff members who are responsive and helpful.

IT'S NEVER TOO LATE

It's never too late to try to help your teenager do well on the test. Some parents think, "Why bother? He's a senior." If you find yourself in this situation, consider the following:

- Senior year is roughly nine months long, and a lot of learning and experience can occur during this time.

- You can always tailor a test-prep plan to fit short-term goals.

- The SAT or ACT is probably not the last standardized test your teenager will take. Students who plan to go on to graduate or professional schools have to take the Graduate Record Exam, the Law School Admission Test, the Medical College Admission Test, or the Graduate Management Admission Test—just to name a few. Many of the same verbal test-taking and test-preparation strategies used for the SAT and ACT also apply to these tests.

- There may be other children in the family who will benefit from this test-prep experience.

- Parent interest keeps both teenagers and teachers on their toes—seniors often need an extra boost during this time to keep their motivation going.

SOME POINTS TO REMEMBER

The purpose of this book has been to help parents prepare their teenagers for, and cope with, college-admissions tests. You're now better prepared to help your teen face the challenge of these tests. As you guide your teen through the test-prep process, keep in the mind the following points:

- Parents and teens need accurate information

- Problems have solutions

- Test-prep plans should emphasize strengths and hone in on problem areas

- Plans should be written down and managed

- The SAT or ACT is one step toward college and career development

YOUR TEEN'S MOST VALUABLE RESOURCE

By now you've learned how to make sure that your teenager's college-admissions test scores really reflect his skills, how to help him improve his performance, and how to feel confident that you have made an important contribution. The key point is that you can help your teenager learn to look ahead and overcome barriers that prevent him from doing his very best. Remember that throughout the process, you are your teenager's most valuable resource. Your attention and involvement will help your teen now at this crucial step and will, later, positively affect your teen's future.

APPENDIX A
SAT Sample Questions and Answers

ESSAY SECTION

Directions: This essay gives you the opportunity to show your effectiveness in developing and expressing your ideas. Consider the following statement.

"Innovation is primarily accomplished by an individual, though groups often do work out the details of an individual's innovations."

Assignment: Write an essay in which you agree or disagree with the preceding statement. Develop your point of view on this statement and be sure to support your stance with sufficient details.

Answer: As you might expect, answers will vary. If possible, ask a teacher, fellow student, or some other person who is knowledgeable about formal essay writing to review your essay and provide feedback on ways in which the essay is commendable and ways in which it could be improved.

MATHEMATICS SECTION

Directions: This section usually contains approximately 20 questions.

1. All numbers used are real numbers.

2. All angle measurements can be assumed to be positive unless otherwise noted.

3. All figures lie in the same plane unless otherwise noted.

4. Drawings that accompany questions are intended to provide information useful in answering the question.

5. The figures are drawn closely to scale unless otherwise noted.

1. What percentage of 75 is 12?

   (A) 8%

   (B) 12%

   (C) 16%

   (D) 18%

   (E) 20%

   The correct answer is (C).

2. Which of the following could have a slope of 1?

   (A)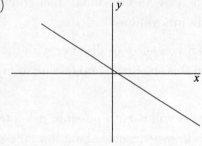

   (C)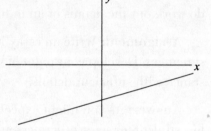

   (B)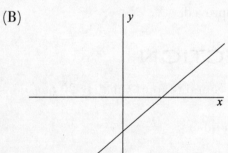

   (D)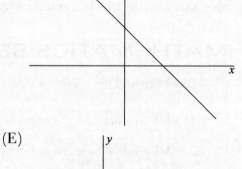

   (E)

   The correct answer is (B).

3. If a circle is inscribed in a square of area 36, what is the area of the circle?

(A) 36π

(B) 24π

(C) 12π

(D) 9π

(E) 6π

The correct answer is (D).

4. The first four terms of a series are 1, 4, 9, and 16. What is the eighth term of this series?

(A) 49

(B) 56

(C) 64

(D) 72

(E) 81

The correct answer is (C).

5. What is the area of the below parallelogram?

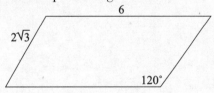

(A) 16

(B) 18

(C) 22

(D) 24

(E) 32

The correct answer is (B).

6. Which of the following fractions has the greatest reciprocal?

(A) $\dfrac{2}{9}$

(B) $\dfrac{4}{5}$

(C) $\dfrac{7}{3}$

(D) $\dfrac{2}{3}$

(E) $\dfrac{3}{13}$

The correct answer is (A).

Directions for Student-Produced Response Questions

Each of the remaining 5 questions requires you to solve the problem and enter your answer by marking the ovals in the special grid, as shown in the examples below.

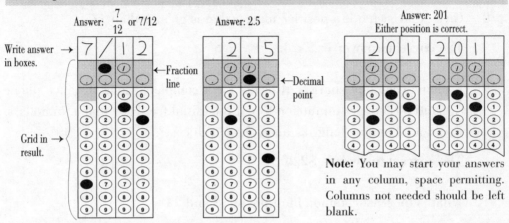

- Mark no more than one oval in any column.

- Because the answer sheet will be machine-scored, **you will receive credit only if the ovals are filled in correctly.**

- Although not required, it is suggested that you write your answer in the boxes at the top of the columns to help you fill in the ovals accurately.

- Some problems may have more than one correct answer. In such cases, grid only one answer.

- No question has a negative answer.

- **Mixed numbers** such as $2\frac{1}{2}$ must be gridded as 2.5 or 5/2. (if 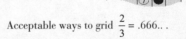 is gridded, it will be interpreted as 21 / 2, not $2\frac{1}{2}$.)

- **Decimal Accuracy:** If you obtain a decimal answer, **enter the most accurate value the grid will accommodate.** For example, if you obtain an answer such as 0.6666 . . ., you should record the result as .666 or .667. **Less accurate values such as .66 and .67 are not acceptable.**

7. $\left[2\left(3^2\right)^2 + \left(4 - 3(4)\right)^2\right] =$

The correct answer is 226.

8. Given that , what is a positive integer that is greater than x?

The correct answer is $x < 3$.

9. A phone company charges 40 cents for a completed long-distance phone call and 6 cents per minute on top of the initial fee. How much, in dollars, would a 30 minute long-distance phone call cost?

The correct answer is $2.20.

10. What is the least common multiple of 18 and 24?

The correct answer is 144.

11. If , then what is one integer value that x cannot equal?

The correct answer is any integer between 1 and 5. The only two positive integers less than 3 are 2 or 1, both acceptable answers.

CRITICAL READING SECTION

Directions: The section usually contains approximately 24 questions. Each of the following questions consists of an incomplete sentence followed by five words or pairs of words. Choose the word or pair of words which, when substituted for the blank space or spaces, best completes the meaning of the sentence as a whole.

1. The professor's oldest colleague was selected to give the ----- at the funeral.

   (A) eulogy

   (B) elegy

   (C) epigraph

   (D) eponymy

   (E) epitaph

   The correct answer is (A).

2. The new team member's ----- was an encouragement to the rest of the team, who had become ----- by the string of defeats.

   (A) enthusiasm . . . elated

   (B) vigor . . . inundated

   (C) ebullience . . . dispirited

   (D) dourness . . . undone

   (E) excessiveness . . . downcast

   The correct answer is (C).

3. By the end of the campaign both candidates had resorted to ----- the other.

   (A) commending

   (B) denigrating

   (C) mollifying

   (D) conceding

   (E) swindling

   The correct answer is (B).

4. The cat ----- crept across the lawn, gracefully ----- the dog.

   (A) felicitously . . . enticing

   (B) swiftly . . . defeating

   (C) acrobatically . . . apprehending

   (D) maladroitly . . . undermining

   (E) deftly . . . eluding

   The correct answer is (E).

5. The storyteller's ----- anecdotes earned her the ----- attention of the crowd.

   (A) compelling . . . rapt

   (B) pointed . . . spellbound

   (C) moribund . . . lucid

   (D) poignant . . . abrasive

   (E) meandering . . . distracted

   The correct answer is (A).

Directions: Answer the questions below based on the information in the accompanying passages.

Musical notes, like all sounds, are a result of the sound waves created by movement, like the rush of air through a trumpet. Musical notes are very regular sound waves. The qualities of these waves—how much they displace molecules, and how often they do so—give the note its
(5) particular sound. How much a sound wave displaces molecules affects the volume of the note. How frequently a sound wave reaches your ear determines whether the note is high- or low-pitched. When scientists describe how high or low a sound is, they use a numerical measurement of its frequency, such as "440 vibrations per second," rather than the
(10) letters musicians use.

6. In this passage, musical notes are used primarily to

(A) illustrate the difference between human-produced and non-human-produced sound.

(B) demonstrate the difference between musical sound and all other sound.

(C) provide an example of sound properties common to all sounds.

(D) convey the difference between musical pitch and frequency pitch.

(E) explain the connection between number and letter names for sounds.

The correct answer is (C).

7. All of the following are true statements about pitch, according to the passage, EXCEPT

   (A) non-musical sounds cannot be referred to in terms of pitch.

   (B) pitch is solely determined by the frequency of the sound wave.

   (C) pitch is closely related to the vibration of molecules.

   (D) pitch cannot be accurately described with letter names.

   (E) humans' perception of pitch is not affected by the intensity of the sound wave.

   The correct answer is (A).

Margaret Walker, who would become one of the most important twentieth-century African-American poets, was born in Birmingham, Alabama, in 1915. Her parents, a minister and a music teacher, encouraged her to read poetry and philosophy even as a child. Walker
(5)   completed her high school education at Gilbert Academy in New Orleans and went on to attend New Orleans University for two years. It was then that the important Harlem Renaissance poet Langston Hughes recognized her talent and persuaded her to continue her education in the North. She transferred to Northwestern University in Illinois, where she
(10)   received a degree in English in 1935. Her poem "For My People," which would remain one of her most important works, was also her first publication, appearing in *Poetry* magazine in 1937.

8. The passage cites Walker's interaction with Langston Hughes as

    (A) instrumental in her early work being published.

    (B) influential in her decision to study at Northwestern University.

    (C) not as important at the time it happened as it is now, due to Hughes' fame.

    (D) a great encouragement for Walker's confidence as a poet.

    (E) important to her choice to study at New Orleans University.

    The correct answer is (B).

9. The passage suggests that Walker's decision to become a poet

    (A) occurred before she entered college.

    (B) was primarily a result of her interaction with Hughes.

    (C) was not surprising, given her upbringing.

    (D) occurred after her transfer to Northwestern University.

    (E) was sudden and immediately successful.

    The correct answer is (C).

Questions 10–11 are based on the following passage.

In 1953, Watson and Crick unlocked the structure of the DNA molecule and set into motion the modern study of genetics. This advance allowed our study of life to go beyond the so-called wet and dirty realm of biology, the complicated laboratory study of proteins, cells, organelles, ions,
(5) and lipids. The study of life could now be performed with more abstract methods of analysis. By discovering the basic structure of DNA, we had received our first glance into the information-based realm locked inside the genetic code.

10. Which of the following does the passage discuss as a change that the discovery of DNA brought to the study of life?

(A) The study of lipids and proteins became irrelevant.

(B) New and more abstract methods of study were possible.

(C) Biology could then focus on molecules rather than cells.

(D) Modern genetics matured past its Mendelian roots.

(E) Information-based study of genes became obsolete.

The correct answer is (B).

11. The passage uses the phrase "wet and dirty" (line 3) to mean

(A) haphazard guessing about the genetic code.

(B) the work of Watson and Crick in discovering DNA.

(C) information-based biological research.

(D) the study of the genetic code.

(E) the involved laboratories practices in studying basic biological entities.

The correct answer is (E).

Questions 12–19 are based on the following passage.

This passage discusses the work of Abe Kobo, a Japanese novelist of the twentieth century.

Abe Kobo is one of the great writers of postwar Japan. His literature is richer, less predictable, and wider-ranging than that of his famed contemporaries, Mishima Yukio and Nobel laureate Oe Kenzaburo. It is infused with the passion and strangeness of his experiences in Manchuria,

(5) which was a Japanese colony on mainland China before World War II. Kobo spent his childhood and much of his youth in Manchuria, and, as a result, the orbit of his work would be far less controlled by the oppressive gravitational pull of the themes of *furusato* (hometown) and the emperor than the work of his contemporaries.

(10) Kobo, like most of the sons of Japanese families living in Manchuria, did return to Japan for schooling. He entered medical school in Tokyo in 1944—just in time to forge himself a medical certificate claiming ill health; this allowed him to avoid fighting in the war that Japan was already losing and return to Manchuria. When Japan lost the war, how-

(15) ever, it also lost its Manchurian colony. The Japanese living there were attacked by the Soviet Army and various guerrilla bands. They suddenly found themselves refugees, desperate for food. Many men who were considered "unfit" were abandoned in the Manchurian desert. At this apocalyptic time, Kobo lost his father to cholera.

(20) He returned to mainland Japan once more, where the young were turning to Marxism as a rejection of the militarism of the war. After a brief, unsuccessful stint at medical school, he became part of a Marxist group of avant-garde artists. His work at this time was passionate and outspoken on political matters, adopting black humor as its mode of

(25) critique. During this time, Kobo worked in the genres of theater, music, and photography. Eventually, he mimeographed fifty copies of his first "published" literary work, entitled *Anonymous Poems*, in 1947. It was a politically-charged set of poems dedicated to the memory of his father

and friends who had died in Manchuria. Shortly thereafter, he published
(30) his first novel, *For a Signpost at the End of a Road*, which imagined
another life for his best friend who had died in the Manchurian desert.

Unfortunately, most of this radical early work is unknown outside
Japan and underappreciated even in Japan. In early 1962, Abe was dis-
missed from the Japanese Liberalist Party. Four months later, he pub-
(35) lished the work that would blind us to his earlier oeuvre, *Woman in the
Dunes*. It was director Teshigahara Hiroshi's film adaptation of *Woman
in the Dunes* that brought Kobo's work to the international stage. The
movie's fame has wrongly led readers to view the novel as Abe's mas-
terpiece. It would be more accurate to say that the novel simply marked
(40) a turning point in his career, when Kobo turned away from the experimental and heavily political work of his earlier career. Fortunately, he
did not then turn to *furusato* and the emperor after all, but rather began
a somewhat more realistic exploration of his continuing obsession with
homelessness and alienation. Not completely a stranger to his earlier
(45) commitment to Marxism, beginning in the sixties, Kobo turned his attention, to the effects on the individual of Japan's rapidly urbanizing,
growth-driven, increasingly corporate society.

12. The word "infused" in line 4 most closely means

    (A) illuminated.

    (B) saturated.

    (C) influenced.

    (D) bewildered.

    (E) nuanced.

The correct answer is (C).

13. The author refers to "the orbit" of Abe's work (line 7) to emphasize that

(A) his work covers a wide range of themes.

(B) the emperor is often compared to a sun.

(C) Abe's travels were the primary themes in his work.

(D) Abe's work is so different from that of his contemporaries that it is like another solar system.

(E) conventional themes can limit an author's individuality.

The correct answer is (E).

14. From the sentence beginning "He entered medical school. . . " in lines 11–14, it can be inferred that

(A) Kobo entered medical school because he was sick.

(B) sick people were sent to Manchuria during World War II.

(C) Kobo wanted to help the ill and injured in World War II, rather than fighting.

(D) illness would excuse one from military duty in World War II Japan.

(E) Abe never intended to practice medicine.

The correct answer is (D).

15. The author uses the word "apocalyptic" to emphasize that

(A) Manchuria suffered intensely as a result of the use of nuclear weapons in World War II.

(B) Kobo was deeply affected by the loss of his father.

(C) there was massive famine in Manchuria at the end of World War II.

(D) post-war Manchuria experienced exhilarating change.

(E) conditions in Manchuria after World War II were generally horrific.

The correct answer is (E).

16. The word "avant-garde" (line 23) could best be replaced by

(A) experimental.

(B) dramatic.

(C) novel.

(D) profound.

(E) realistic.

The correct answer is (A).

17. Which of the following does the passage present as a fact?

(A) Kobo was a better playwright than novelist.

(B) Kobo's early work was of greater quality than his later work.

(C) The group of avant-garde artists of which Kobo was a part were influenced by Marxism.

(D) The themes of *furusato* and the emperor have precluded Japanese literature from playing a major role in world literature.

(E) Kobo's work is richer than that of his contemporaries because he included autobiographical elements.

The correct answer is (C).

18. The phrase "blind us" in line 35 refers to the

(A) absence of film adaptations for Kobo's other novels.

(B) excessive critical attention to Kobo's novel, *Woman in the Dunes*.

(C) difficulty in reconciling *Woman in the Dunes* and other later works with the form and content of his earlier works.

(D) challenge of interpreting Kobo's more experimental works.

(E) overwhelming power of Kobo's novel, *Woman in the Dunes*.

The correct answer is (B).

19. The author's main purpose in the passage is to

(A) defend Kobo's later works against the prevalent criticism of it.

(B) advocate for Kobo's work over that of his contemporaries.

(C) explain the differences between Kobo's earlier and later works.

(D) argue that Kobo is an even greater writer and artist than generally perceived.

(E) demonstrate that Kobo's work became less interesting after he left Manchuria.

The correct answer is (D).

WRITING SECTION

Directions: This section usually contains approximately 35 questions. For each question, choose the best answer from the choices given. The following questions test your knowledge of English grammar, word usage, word choice, sentence construction, and punctuation. Every sentence contains a portion that is underlined. Any errors that occur will be found in the underlined portion of the sentence. If you believe there is an error, choose the answer choice that corrects the original mistake. Answer choices (B), (C), (D), and (E) contain alternative phrasings of the underlined portion. For those sentences with an error, one of these alternate phrasings will use the correct words to express the original sentence's meaning. Choice (A) repeats the original underlined portion. If you believe the underlined portion does not contain any errors, pick answer choice (A).

1. <u>Her first novel having been published</u>, the author began to take notes for her second.

    (A) Her first novel having been published

    (B) Having been her most recent novel published

    (C) Her first novel, having been published

    (D) When having had her first novel published

    (E) Having published her first novel

    The correct answer is (E).

2. Van Gogh's early work has often been described as being in sharp contrast with his later <u>work, despite</u> there is a fundamental continuity between the two.

    (A) later work, despite

    (B) work; despite the fact that

    (C) work, rather,

    (D) work, but

    (E) work, notwithstanding

    The correct answer is (D).

3. <u>After working on his serve for several days, rumors circulated that the challenger would win the rematch</u>.

   (A) After working on his serve for several days, rumors circulated that the challenger would win the rematch.

   (B) After working on his serve for several days, the challenger circulated rumors that he would win the rematch.

   (C) Rumors circulated that the challenger, after working on his serve for several days, would win the rematch.

   (D) After having worked on his serve for several days, the rematch was rumored to be won by the challenger.

   (E) After working on his serve for several days, rumors circulated, the challenger would win the rematch.

   The correct answer is (C).

4. The artist thought that it was important both to portray the subject truthfully, no matter the difficulty, <u>and revealing something new about the subject.</u>

   (A) and revealing something new about the subject.

   (B) and so he revealed something new about the subject.

   (C) and to reveal something new about the subject.

   (D) having thereby revealed something new about the subject.

   (E) and revealing something about the subject that is new.

   The correct answer is (C).

5. Max Planck was not only one of the founders of quantum <u>mechanics, but an accomplished pianist.</u>

   (A) mechanics, but an accomplished pianist.

   (B) mechanics; but he was also an accomplished pianist.

   (C) mechanics; and he was also an accomplished pianist.

   (D) mechanics, and an accomplished pianist.

   (E) mechanics, but also an accomplished piano.

   The correct answer is (B).

Directions:

1. The following questions test your knowledge of the rules of English grammar, as well as word usage, word choice, and idioms.

2. Some sentences are correct, but others contain a single error. No sentence contains more than one error.

3. Any errors that occur will be found in the underlined portion of the sentence. Choose the letter underneath the error to indicate the part of the sentence that must be changed.

4. If there is no error, pick answer choice (E).

5. There will no change in any parts of the sentence that are not underlined.

6. Despite the enormous voter drive, there are still many city-dwellers who
   (A)   (B)   (C)
   are not registered to vote. No error
           (D)   (E)

   The correct answer is (E).

7. Debating the energy bill was the first order of business for the Senate; to set
   (A)   (B)   (C)
   the calendar for the upcoming session was to follow. No error
                                           (D)   (E)

   The correct answer is (C).

8. The FDA did not conclude that the negative side affects of the drug offset
                (A)   (B)   (C)
   the drug's positive benefits. No error
                        (D)   (E)

   The correct answer is (B).

9. Over the last <u>decade,</u> the information industry <u>had grown</u> into a multi-bil-
           (A)   (B)
    lion dollar industry <u>that</u> <u>employs</u> tens of thousands of workers. <u>No error</u>
                         (C)   (D)   (E)

    The correct answer is (B).

10. <u>Reading widely</u> in her field, <u>making herself</u> available to students, and
       (A)   (B)

    <u>her sophisticated research</u> <u>paid off for</u> Professor Jackson: she was awarded
           (C)   (D)

    tenure last year. <u>No error</u>
                 (E)

    The correct answer is (C).

Directions: The following questions test your knowledge of paragraph and sentence construction. The following passage is a rough draft of an essay. This rough draft contains various errors. Read the rough draft and then answer the questions that follow. Some questions will focus on specific sentences and ask if there are any problems with that sentence's word choice, word usage, or overall structure. Other questions will ask about the paragraph itself. These questions will focus on paragraph organization and development.

Questions 11–15 are based on the following passage.

(1) An incredible hot-air balloon exhibition happened on September 5, 1862. (2) It was given by Glaisher and Coxwell, two Englishmen. (3) There was no compressed oxygen for them to breathe in those days. (4) They got so high that they couldn't use their limbs. (5) Coxwell had to open the descending valve with his teeth. (6) Before Glaisher passed out, he recorded an elevation of twenty-nine thousand feet. (7) Many believe they got eight thousand feet higher before they began to descend, making their ascent the highest in the nineteenth century.

(5)

(8) Now the largest balloon to go up in the nineteenth century was "The Giant." (9) The balloon held 215,000 cubic feet of air and was 74 feet wide. (10) It could carry four and a half tons of cargo. (11) Its

(10)

flight began in Paris, in 1853, with fifteen passengers. (12) All of whom
returned safely. (13) The successful trip received a great deal of national
and international press because many thought the hot-air balloon would
(15) become a form of common transportation.

11. Which of the following offers the best combination of sentences 1 and 2
(reproduced below)?

*An incredible hot-air balloon exhibition happened on September 5, 1862.
It was given by Glaisher and Coxwell, two Englishmen.*

(A) An incredible hot-air balloon exhibition was given September 5, 1962
by Glaisher and Coxwell, two Englishmen.

(B) An incredibly hot air balloon exhibition happened on September 5,
1862, given by Glaisher and Coxwell, two Englishmen.

(C) Given by Glaisher and Coxwell, two Englishmen, an incredible hot-air
balloon exhibition happened on September 5, 1862.

(D) Glaisher and Coxwell, two Englishmen, gave an incredible hot-air
balloon exhibition, happening on September 5, 1862.

(E) Two Englishmen, Glaisher and Coxwell, gave an incredible hot-air
balloon exhibition on September 5, 1862.

The correct answer is (E).

12. Which of the following sentences in the first paragraph appears to be out of
order?

(A) There was no compressed oxygen for them to breathe in those days.

(B) They got so high that they couldn't use their limbs.

(C) Coxwell had to open the descending valve with his teeth.

(D) Before Glaisher passed out, he recorded an elevation of twenty-nine
thousand feet.

(E) Many believe they got eight thousand feet higher before they began to
descend.

The correct answer is (A).

13. Which of the following is the best revision for sentence 8 (reproduced below)?

Now the largest balloon to go up in the nineteenth century was "The Giant."

(A) Move "in the nineteenth century" to the beginning of the sentence and delete "Now"

(B) Add a comma after "Now"

(C) Begin the sentence with "Moreover,"

(D) Delete "now"

(E) Replace "to go up" with "exhibition"

The correct answer is (D).

14. Which of the following is the best way to combine sentences 9 and 10 (reproduced below)?

The balloon held 215,000 cubic feet of air and was 74 feet wide. It could handle four and a half tons of cargo.

(A) The balloon held 215,000 cubic feet of air and was 74 feet wide, which could handle four and a half tons of cargo.

(B) The balloon held 215,000 cubic feet of air and was 74 feet wide, handling four and a half tons of cargo.

(C) The balloon held 215,000 cubic feet of air and was 74 feet wide; it could handle four and a half tons of cargo.

(D) The balloon held 215,000 cubic feet of air and was 74 feet wide, and it could handle four and a half tons of cargo.

(E) The balloon held 215,000 cubic feet of air and was 74 feet wide, but it could carry four and a half tons of cargo.

The correct answer is (C).

15. Which of the following is the best way to revise the underlined portions of sentences 11 and 12 (reproduced below)?

Its flight began in Paris, in 1853, <u>with fifteen passengers. All of whom returned safely</u>.

(A) Replace "whom" with "who"

(B) Make the second sentence read "Who all returned safely."

(C) Delete "of"

(D) Replace the period at the end of sentence 11 with a comma

(E) Delete the period and change "returned" to "returning"

The correct answer is (D).

APPENDIX B
ACT Sample Questions and Answers

ENGLISH SECTION

Directions: This section usually consists of five passages in which particular words or phrases are underlined and numbered. Questions following the passage will present alternative words and phrases that could be substituted for the underlined part. Select the alternative that expresses the idea most clearly and correctly or that best fits the style and tone of the entire passage. If the original version is best, select "No Change."

The section also includes questions about entire paragraphs and the passage as a whole. These questions are identified by a number in a box.

   After you select the correct answer for each question, on your answer sheet, mark the oval corresponding to the correct answer.

Passage—The Girls Choir of Harlem

It is rare to hear of choirs composed of <u>just girls.</u> In fact, for every girls'
                                                    1
choir in the United States, <u>there are ten choirs that are boys' or mixed.</u>
                                                                          2
But, in 1977, the Girls Choir of Harlem was founded to complement

<u>the already existing</u> and justly renowned Boys Choir.
        3

To this day, the Boys Choir of Harlem overshadows the Girls Choir. It had been around longer since 1968 and has received the attention needed to
   4   5
gain funding and performance opportunities. The boys have appeared in some of the world's most prestigious musical settings. Performing a sunrise concert
                                6
for the Pope on the Great Lawn in New York's Central Park, and they have traveled to Washington, D.C. where in front of the reflecting pool they sung in
                                     7
front of the Washington monument.

[8] During the 1980s, when funds dried up, the Girls Choir temporarily disbanded. However, in 1989, the choir reassembled, and in November of 1997, they made their debut at Alice Tully Hall at Lincoln Center, performing music by Schumann and Pergolesi toward the audience of dignitaries, includ-
                          9
ing the mayor's wife and thousands of music lovers.
              10

Giving kids from broken families and poverty-stricken homes new con-
  11
fidence and hope for their future, both the Girls Choir and the Boys Choir of Harlem act as havens for inner-city children. The boys and girls in the choirs attend the Choir Academy. The 500-student public school strongly em-phasizes singing. [12] It's a fine learning environment that has given the girls ambitions most of them never before considered. The choir members speak confidently of someday becoming lawyers, doctors, and politicians—jobs appearing out of reach to them.
  13

Now that the Girls Choir of Harlem is receiving some of the recognition that the boys have long enjoyed, perhaps corporations and wealthy individuals will be motivated to give generously to support the choir and ensure it will never again <u>be canceled</u> for lack of money. |15|
14

1. (A) NO CHANGE
   (B) only just girls.
   (C) girls alone.
   (D) girls and no boys.
   The correct answer is (A).

2. (F) NO CHANGE
   (G) ten are either boys' or mixed choirs.
   (H) each of ten choirs are either boys' or mixed.
   (J) there are ten that are either boys' or mixed choirs.
   The correct answer is (J).

3. (A) NO CHANGE
   (B) what already existed
   (C) the existing
   (D) already existing
   The correct answer is (A).

4. (F) NO CHANGE
   (G) was
   (H) has been
   (J) being
   The correct answer is (H).

5. (A) NO CHANGE

    (B) longer, since 1968 and

    (C) longer since 1968, and

    (D) longer (since 1968) and

    The correct answer is (D).

6. (F) NO CHANGE

    (G) They have performed

    (H) A performance of

    (J) The choir performs

    The correct answer is (G).

7. (A) NO CHANGE

    (B) they sung in front of the reflecting pool

    (C) before the reflecting pool they sung

    (D) they sung at the reflecting pool

    The correct answer is (D).

8. Which of the following sentences provides the most effective transition from the previous paragraph to this one?

    (F) Such glorious moments eluded their female counterparts, at least at first.

    (G) The Boys Choir and Girls Choir both have performed mainly in the Northeastern part of the United States.

    (H) The Girls Choir, though not as experienced as the Boys Choir, is considered equally talented.

    (J) The Boys Choir was able to attract more funding than the Girls Choir.

    The correct answer is (F).

9. (A) NO CHANGE

   (B) before an

   (C) in front of the

   (D) at an

   The correct answer is (B).

10. (F) NO CHANGE

    (G) wife, and

    (H) wife as well as

    (J) wife, along with

    The correct answer is (G).

11. (A) NO CHANGE

    (B) They give

    (C) By giving

    (D) As they give

    The correct answer is (C).

12. Which of the following sentences, if inserted at this point in the essay, would be most logical and appropriate?

    (F) Nevertheless, it provides a well-rounded education that helps prepare students for a variety of careers.

    (G) Classes in vocal technique, sight reading, and even music theory are all part of the regular curriculum.

    (H) The student body is carefully selected from a much larger pool of applicants.

    (J) Students are admitted based on financial need as well as their musical abilities, especially their singing ability.

    The correct answer is (F).

13. (A) NO CHANGE

     (B) appeared

     (C) that once appeared

     (D) that would have appeared

     The correct answer is (C).

14. (F) NO CHANGE

     (G) close its doors

     (H) stop what they do

     (J) go silent

     The correct answer is (J).

Item 15 poses a question about the essay as a whole.

15. Suppose the writer had been assigned to write an essay describing the musical achievements of the Girls Choir of Harlem. Would this essay successfully fulfill the assignment?

     (A) Yes, because the essay makes it clear that the girls in the choir are talented performers.

     (B) Yes, because the concert at Alice Tully Hall is explained in some detail.

     (C) No, because the music performed by the choir is scarcely discussed in the essay.

     (D) No, because the essay discusses the Boys Choir as extensively as the Girls Choir.

     The correct answer is (C).

MATHEMATICS SECTION

Directions: Solve each problem. Be careful not to spend too much time on any one question. Instead, solve as many problems as possible, and then use the remaining time to return to those questions you were unable to answer at first.

You may use a calculator on any problem in this section. However, some problems can best be solved without use of a calculator.

Note: Unless otherwise stated, you can assume that:

1. Diagrams that accompany problems are not necessarily drawn to scale.
2. All figures lie in the same plane.
3. The word "line" refers to a straight line (and lines that appear straight are straight).
4. The word "average" refers to arithmetic mean.

1. The number 40.5 is 1,000 times larger than which of the following numbers?

(A) .405

(B) .0405

(C) .0450

(D) .00405

(E) .000405

The correct answer is (B).

2. If the length, width, and height of a cube measuring 2 centimeters along each edge are each increased by 50%, what is the resulting increase in the cube's volume, expressed in cubic centimeters?

   (F) 27

   (G) 24

   (H) 19

   (J) 16

   (K) 12

   The correct answer is (H).

3. If x is a real number, and if $x^3 = 100$, then x lies between which two consecutive integers?

   (A) 1 and 2

   (B) 2 and 3

   (C) 3 and 4

   (D) 4 and 5

   (E) 5 and 6

   The correct answer is (D).

4. Lyle's current age is 23 years, and Melanie's current age is 15 years. How many years ago was Lyle's age twice Melanie's age?

   (F) 16

   (G) 9

   (H) 8

   (J) 7

   (K) 5

   The correct answer is (J).

5. A certain zoo charges exactly twice as much for an adult admission ticket as for a child's admission ticket. If the total admission price for the family of two adults and two children is $12.60, what is the price of a child's ticket?

(A) $1.60

(B) $2.10

(C) $3.20

(D) $3.30

(E) $4.20

The correct answer is (B).

6. One marble is to be drawn randomly from a bag that contains three red marbles, two blue marbles, and one green marble. What is the probability of drawing a blue marble?

(F) $\frac{1}{6}$

(G) $\frac{1}{5}$

(H) $\frac{2}{7}$

(J) $\frac{1}{3}$

(K) $\frac{2}{5}$

The correct answer is (J).

7. Point A bisects line segment $\overline{BC}$, and point D bisects line segment $\overline{BA}$. Which of the following congruencies holds?

(A) $\overline{DC} \cong \overline{CB}$

(B) $\overline{BA} \cong \overline{CB}$

(C) $\overline{DC} \cong \overline{DA}$

(D) $\overline{AD} \cong \overline{DB}$

(E) $\overline{CA} \cong \overline{BC}$

The correct answer is (D).

8. If $\dfrac{2y}{9} = \dfrac{y-1}{3}$, then $y =$

(F) $\dfrac{1}{3}$

(G) $\dfrac{3}{5}$

(H) $\dfrac{4}{9}$

(J) $\dfrac{9}{4}$

(K) 3

The correct answer is (K).

9. $4\dfrac{1}{2} + 3\dfrac{3}{4} - 2\dfrac{2}{5} =$

(A) $\dfrac{57}{10}$

(B) $\dfrac{231}{40}$

(C) $\dfrac{117}{20}$

(D) $\dfrac{23}{4}$

(E) $\dfrac{29}{5}$

The correct answer is (C).

10. If $a = 3$, $b = -3$, and $c = \dfrac{1}{3}$, then $ab^2c^2 =$

(F) -27

(G) -1

(H) 3

(J) 9

(K) 27

The correct answer is (J).

READING SECTION

Directions: This section usually consists of several passages, each followed by questions. Read each passage and select the best answer for each question following the passage.

Passage—Social Studies

When the framers of the Constitution set to work devising the structure of the U.S. government, it was natural for them to consider the forms already existing in the several states. The three most basic patterns may be referred to as the Virginia, Pennsylvania, and Massachusetts models.

(5)   The Virginia model borrowed its central principle, legislative supremacy, from the thinking of the English philosopher John Locke. Locke had favored making the legislature the dominant focus of government power, and he stressed the importance of preventing a monarch, governor, or other executive from usurping that power. In line with Locke's doctrine,
(10) Virginia's constitution provided that the governor be chosen by the assembly rather than by the people directly, as were the members of a special governor's council. The approval of this council was necessary for any action by the governor.

    Also derived from Locke was Virginia's bicameral legislature, in which
(15) both chambers must concur to pass a bill. Thus dividing the legislative power was supposed to prove its domination by any single faction—the so-called "division of powers" which later became an important feature of the national constitution.

    Pennsylvania's constitution was probably the most democratic of any
(20) in the former colonies. Pennsylvania extended the right to vote to most adult males. (With the exception of Vermont, the other states allowed only property owners to vote; New Jersey alone extended the privilege to women.) Pennsylvanians elected the members of a single-house legis-

lature, as well as an executive council. These bodies jointly selected the
(25) council president, who served as the state's chief executive officer; there
was no governor. Neither legislators nor council members could remain
in office more than four years out of seven.

The most conservative of the models was found in Massachusetts. The
legislature here included two chambers. In the House of Representatives,
(30) the number of legislators for a given district was based on population;
in the "aristocratic" senate, representation was based on taxable wealth.
The governor could veto legislature, he appointed most state officials,
and he was elected independently of the legislature.

As the delegates to the Constitutional Convention began to debate the
(35) merits of these varying models, several fault lines began to appear along
which the representatives of the former colonies were divided. One such
line was geographic. The economic and social differences between the
northern and southern states, which would lead, three generations later,
to the cataclysm of the Civil War, were already making themselves felt.
(40) Dependent chiefly on the export of such raw materials as cotton, tobacco,
and rice, the southern states strongly opposed giving Congress the power
to regulate international trade, fearing the imposition of onerous taxes
or tariffs. Also, the white slaveholders of the south feared federal restric-
tions on the practice of slavery, which was already a point of controversy
(45) between sections of the new nation.

Another dividing line among the states was based on population. The
less populous states opposed the notion of allocating political power based
on population; they feared having the larger states, especially Virginia,
New York, Massachusetts, and Pennsylvania, ride roughshod over their
(50) interests. This division to some extent echoed the north-south split, since
most of the more populous states were in the north.

The debates over governmental structure quickly focused on the
makeup of the legislative branch. The most populous states favored
making representation in Congress proportional to population, while the

(55) smaller states fought for equality of representation. For a time, it appeared as though the convention might break up over this issue.

The successful resolution was a compromise originally proposed by the delegation from Connecticut, and therefore often referred to as the Connecticut Compromise, or the Great Compromise. According to this *(60)* plan, which remains in effect to this day, the Congress is a bicameral legislature like those in Virginia and Massachusetts. In the Senate, each state has two representatives, no matter what its size, while seats in the House of Representatives are apportioned by population. Both houses must concur in the passage of legislature, and bills proposing the expen- *(65)* diture of government funds must originate in the House—a precaution demanded by the larger states to protect their financial interests.

The southern states won a series of specific concessions. Although the convention refused to include slaves on an equal basis in the population count for Congressional representation—after all, the slaves were nei- *(70)* ther citizens nor taxpayers nor voters—it was agreed to count the slave population, a notorious compromise long regarded as a racist blot on the constitution. The north also accepted constitutional clauses forbidding export taxes and preventing Congress from interfering with the slave trade until at least 1808—more than twenty years in the future. The *(75)* sectional differences between north and south, and the simmering issue of slavery, were thus postponed for future generations to face.

1. Based on the passage, under which government model did the governor hold the most extensive powers?

   (A) Pennsylvania

   (B) Washington

   (C) Massachusetts

   (D) Virginia

   The correct answer is (C).

2. It can most reasonably be inferred that "larger states" (line 48) refers to the states that were:

(F) wealthiest.

(G) largest in geographic size.

(H) most powerful.

(J) most populous.

The correct answer is (H).

3. As it is used in the passage, the word *onerous* (line 42) most nearly means:

(A) beneficial.

(B) burdensome.

(C) unnecessary.

(D) useless.

The correct answer is (B).

4. Which of the following former colonies mentioned in the passage was most strongly influenced by the philosophy of John Locke?

(F) Virginia

(G) Pennsylvania

(H) Massachusetts

(J) New Jersey

The correct answer is (F).

5. As a whole, the passage is best viewed as a(n):

(A) account of how former colonizers devised an effective model of self-governance for the newly independent colonies.

(B) explanation of how pre-existing patterns of governance in the original states influenced the constitution of those states newly united as a nation.

(C) study of how the framers of the U.S. Constitution ultimately solved the problems arising from political and economic differences between the Northern and Southern states.

(D) discourse on the influence of diverse political philosophies on the framers of the U.S. Constitution.

The correct answer is (B).

6. Based on the passage, which of the following models of a constitution would an adherent of Locke's philosophy most likely prefer?

(F) A constitution that calls for a governing body comprised of two chambers and a jointly selected chief executive officer

(G) A conservative constitution that provides for a government made up of representatives based on their taxable wealth

(H) A constitution requiring the agreement of both chambers to pass any draft of a proposed law

(J) A democratic constitution under which the nominated head of the two chambers holds veto power, for the purpose of avoiding dominance by any particular faction

The correct answer is (H).

7. It can be inferred from the passage that the representatives of the southern states were concerned with protecting the interests of all of the following EXCEPT:

(A) regulators of international trade.

(B) owners of cotton-producing plantations.

(C) white slave holders.

(D) exporters of tobacco.

The correct answer is (A).

8. The northern states strongly supported the constitutional provision that:

(F) prohibited export taxes.

(G) prohibited Congressional interference in the slave trade.

(H) required that all funding bills originate in the House of Representatives.

(J) called for equal representation of all states in the Senate.

The correct answer is (H).

9. In what way did the constitution of New Jersey differ from those of the other states?

(A) It was the only state to confer the right to vote on slaves.

(B) It gave women the privilege to vote.

(C) It conferred the right to vote exclusively to property holders.

(D) Seats in its legislature were given exclusively to taxpayers.

The correct answer is (B).

10. The passage supports all of the following ideas EXCEPT:

(F) the debate over how Congressional seats should be apportioned nearly resulted in the failure of the Constitutional Convention.

(G) the debate over how the new government was to be structured included the issue of how funding bills should be proposed.

(H) the question of the legality of slavery in a democracy was left largely unaddressed by the Constitutional Convention.

(J) all major differences between the Northern and Southern states were settled by the time the new Constitution was finally adopted.

The correct answer is (J).

SCIENCE REASONING SECTION

Directions: This section usually consists of several passages, each followed by questions. Read each passage and select the best answer for each question following the passage.

Passage

Biologists have discovered certain genes (the basic unit of genetic material found on the chromosomes) that behave very differently depending on whether they are passed down to offspring from the father or the mother. These genes, called imprinted genes, are chemically altered in cells that give rise to eggs and sperm. These alterations result in dramatically different properties. In the imprinted genes that have been most fully studied, the female alters the gene so that certain proteins are not produced. The protein remains active in the father's genes. Researchers have posed numerous theories to explain the evolution of imprinted genes. Three of the theories are presented below.

Competing Parental Interest Theory

Some biologists think that imprinted genes evolved in a battle between the sexes to determine the size of offspring. It is to the genetic advantage of the female to rear a number of offspring, all of which will pass along her genetic material. Consequently, while she wants each offspring to be healthy, she does not want them to be so large that the strain of feeding and/or delivering them would jeopardize her ability to bear future babies.

Conversely, it is to the genetic advantage of males in non-monogamous species (species that do not always mate for life) to have the mother expend as much of her resources as possible to ensure the health of his offspring. He is not concerned with her ability to bear future offspring, since these will not necessarily be fathered by him (and, therefore, will not be transmitting his genetic material.) Hence, imprinted genes have developed in this parental tug-of-war. Normally, each offspring receives one copy of an imprinted gene from the father and one from the mother. The changes that the parents make in their genes result in an offspring that is smaller than the male would like and larger than the female would like.

Anti-Cancer Theory

This theory holds that imprinted genes evolved to prevent cancer. The genes have been found in the placenta (an organ that develops to nourish a growing fetus). Placental tissue grows and burrows into the uterus, where the fetus develops. The ability to grow and invade tissues is also seen in aggressive cancers. Imprinted genes might have developed to ensure that the potentially dangerous placenta will not develop if there is no fetus to nourish. The female might inactivate certain growth genes in her eggs, while the sperm kept them turned on. If no fertilization took place, the growth would not occur. If a sperm did join the egg, the male's gene would ensure that the protein developed.

Protein Control Theory

A third group of biologists holds that imprinted genes developed to ensure the precise regulation of certain proteins. Genes do their work by initiating the production of different proteins. Some proteins involved in the growth of embryos may need to be regulated with great precision to ensure the healthy development of the offspring. Proponents of the protein control theory suggest that this careful regulation might be easier if only one parent is involved. Thus, one parent might turn off such genes, leaving the regulation to the other.

1. Which of the following experimental findings poses the most serious difficulties for proponents of the anti-cancer theory?

   (A) When a mouse was genetically engineered so that it contained two copies of every gene from its mother only, the embryo was unable to develop.

   (B) Research in animals that lay eggs has never turned up an imprinted gene.

   (C) Imprinted genes have been found in plants, which have no placentas.

   (D) Research has shown that imprinted genes have not evolved as rapidly as they usually do in competitive situations.

   The correct answer is (C).

2. Supporters of the protein control theory believe that:

   (F) imprinted genes are used to regulate crucial proteins.

   (G) imprinted genes are active only in females.

   (H) imprinted genes should not be found in monogamous species (ones that mate for life).

   (J) only the male passes down imprinted genes to the offspring.

   The correct answer is (F).

3. Supporters of the competing parental interest theory assume that:

   (A) only females have an interest in regulating the size of their offspring.

   (B) only males have an interest in ensuring the health and survival of their offspring.

   (C) both males and females have an interest in producing as many offspring of their own sex as possible.

   (D) both males and females have an interest in transmitting their genetic material to as many offspring as possible.

   The correct answer is (D).

4. Supporters of all three theories would agree that:

(F) imprinted genes evolved as a means of regulating reproduction-related events.

(G) imprinted genes should be absent in non-placental animals (animals whose offspring develop without a placenta).

(H) if an embryo is formed without female-imprinted genes, the future ability of the mother to bear offspring will be jeopardized.

(J) imprinted genes should always be turned off in the mother.

The correct answer is (F).

5. Which of the following findings is best explained by the competing parental interest theory?

(A) An imprinted gene has been discovered in humans that appears to influence a child's social skills.

(B) In the imprinted genes that have been most fully studied, the female turns the gene off, while the male's gene remains active.

(C) Studies with a monogamous mouse species indicate that imprinted genes are not active.

(D) One of the imprinted genes studied is known to control a growth-stimulating hormone.

The correct answer is (C).

6. Researchers conducted breeding studies with two species of mice. Species A was monogamous, while Species B was not. Supporters of the competing parental interest theory hypothesized that the monogamous species was unlikely to have active imprinted genes (since the fathers would have the same genetic stake in all the offspring born). Which of the following experimental results would they expect?

(F) When females from Species A were bred with males from Species B, the resulting offspring were extremely small.

(G) When females from Species A were bred with males from Species B, the resulting offspring were extremely large.

(H) When females from Species B were bred with males from Species A, the resulting offspring were extremely large.

(J) The offspring of Species B mice were consistently smaller than the offspring of Species A mice.

The correct answer is (G).

LIST OF RESOURCES

Use the following list of Thomson Peterson's resources to guide you and your teen through the college-admissions process.

Test Preparation

ARCO Master the New SAT. 2004.

Complete coverage of math and verbal skills for the new SAT, with an entire chapter devoted to the new timed essay and with numerous practice questions and drills for Algebra II.

ARCO Panic Plan for the SAT. 2004.

How to ace the new SAT in as little as two weeks—this is the ideal guide for the last-minute studier.

Peterson's ACT Assessment for Brainiacs. 2003.

For high school students who want top scores, this guide explores the most challenging concepts and problems on the assessment.

Peterson's Ultimate ACT Tool Kit 2005. 2004.

This multimedia test-prep regimen has ACT preparation down to an art, with the inside scoop on the optional Writing Test, 5 full-length practice tests, a CD, and online features.

Peterson's Ultimate New SAT Tool Kit 2005. 2004.

After completing a diagnostic test that highlights test areas that require the most concentration, students select the tools that work best for them—5 full-length practice tests, SAT vocabulary flash cards, online essay-scoring, and math e-tutoring.

The Real ACT Prep Guide. 2004.

The ONLY ACT guide with 3 real ACT tests—written by the test-makers of the ACT!

www.petersons.com/testprepchannel/college_bound.asp

Everything you need to get the score you want!

Critical Reading

Get Wise! Mastering Reading Comprehension Skills. 2003.

Clever, wisecracking Chi instructs students on reading wiser—for speed and retention of information—whether they're preparing for standardized tests or daily school assignments.

Peterson's New SAT Critical Reading Workbook. 2004.

With its easy-to-read, interactive format, students using this guide have access to 3 full-length practice Critical Reading sections, 1,000 additional practice problems, and a diagnostic pretest.

Peterson's In-A-Flash Vocabulary. 2003.

With 360 words you need to know for high scores on the SAT and ACT, this is a quick study guide for improving test scores.

Peterson's Success with Words. 2004.

Geared toward students facing the ACT and SAT, this guide teaches them how to speak the tests' language.

Math

Get Wise! Mastering Math Word Problems. 2004.

Word problems don't have to freak you out. Here again you'll find Chi teaching cool lessons and activities for middle and high school students.

Peterson's In-A-Flash Math. 2003.

Build your skills for the SAT and ACT—everything you need to improve your score. Quick, easy, and at your fingertips!

Peterson's New SAT Math Workbook. 2004.

This workbook addresses all the new concepts, such as Algebra II, as well as topics that haven't changed.

Peterson's Ultimate Math Success. 2003.

With a thorough review of all important math concepts, students will be able to boost their test scores with hundreds of practice questions and tips for improving their test-taking speed and accuracy.

Writing

Get Wise! Mastering Grammar Skills. 2002.

This book helps readers improve their grammar for standardized tests, college-admissions exams, and schoolwork.

Get Wise! Mastering Writing Skills. 2002.

Many kids don't enjoy writing. This book will get them to love it by unraveling the wide variety of writing assignments students will encounter in the classroom and on standardized tests.

Peterson's New SAT Writing Workbook. 2004.

With expert strategies and extensive practice, this is the only study guide specifically for the new SAT Writing Test.

www.essayedge.com

Named "the world's premier application-essay editing service" by *The New York Times Learning Network* and "one of the best essay services on the Internet" by *The Washington Post,* EssayEdge has helped more applicants write successful personal statements than any other company in the world.

About College

Boyer, P. *College Rankings Exposed: Getting Beyond the Rankings Myth to Find Your Perfect College.* 2004.

In this groundbreaking book, students and parents are empowered to move beyond catch phrases, leave the numbers behind, and reclaim their search for the right educational fit.

Chatfield, C. *Financial Aid 101.* 2004.

A complete and up-to-date crash course for parents and students on the complex financial-aid process.

Gottesman, G., and Baer, D. *College Survival.* 2004.

While it includes helpful advice on academics and testing, this guide really focuses on the important stuff—like dating, parties, and getting along with roommates—that can make or break a freshman-year experience.

Peterson's Colleges for Students with Learning Disabilities or ADD. 2003.

Updated with all-new information on more than 750 institutions' learning-disability programs, members of the Association on Higher Education and Disability (AHEAD), an international organization of professionals committed to higher education of people with disabilities, contributed to the publication of this guide.

Peterson's Competitive Colleges 2005. 2004.

A selective college guide for high-achieving students, this is the perfect starting point for the motivated student seeking a challenging collegiate experience.

Peterson's Four-Year Colleges 2005. 2004.

The most information-packed college guide available, with details on every accredited four-year college in the United States and Canada.

Peterson's Scholarships, Grants & Prizes 2005. 2004.

With up-to-date information on nearly 1.6 million scholarships worth more than $6 billion, this authoritative guide to private financial aid has something for everyone!

Best College Admissions Essays. Stewart, M., and Muchnick, C. 2004.

This handy step-by-step guide shows students what to do—and what not to do!—in wowing admissions officers with an unforgettable essay.

www.petersons.com

Visit the Internet's most comprehensive education-related site for test preparation and guidance on college admission and financial aid.

LB2353 .S7 .P475 2005 Burke

Oram, Fern
   Peterson's parent's
guide to the SAT & ACT

Your Everything Education Destination...

Petersons.com

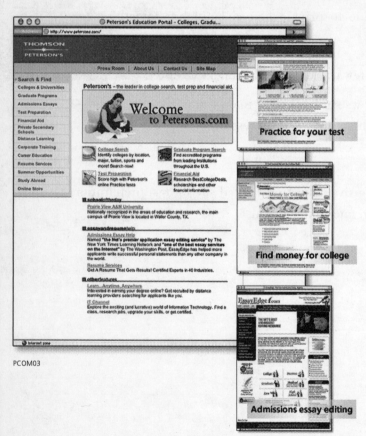

PCOM03

No matter where you're headed, visit the Net's largest, most important education portal.

Whether you're preparing for college, grad school, professional school, or the working world, Petersons.com is your first choice for accurate information and real-world advice.

- Search for the right school
- Find a scholarship
- Take practice admissions tests
- Use interactive courses designed just for you
- Write a better admissions essay with help from Harvard-educated editors

It's your future.
Visit **www.petersons.com** today!

Get **20% off** any book at
Peterson's Online Bookstore

www.petersons.com   Educational Search   Test Preparation   Financial Aid